How to avoid an unnecessary caesarean

A HANDBOOK FOR WOMEN WHO WANT A NATURAL BIRTH

How to avoid an unnecessary caesarean

A HANDBOOK FOR WOMEN WHO WANT A NATURAL BIRTH

Helen Churchill and Wendy Savage

Middlesex University PRESS

First published in 2008 by Middlesex University Press

Copyright © Helen Churchill

ISBN: 978 1 904750 16 1

A CIP catalogue record for this book is available from
The British Library

Design by Helen Taylor

Printed in the UK by Ashford Colour Press

Middlesex University Press
North London Business Park
Oakleigh Road South
London N11 1QS

Tel: +44 (0)20 8411 4162
Fax: +44 (0)20 8411 4167

www.mupress.co.uk

Contents

Introduction

When a caesarean is necessary it can be life saving for mother and baby. However, we have written this handbook because we are of the opinion that many caesareans are being performed unnecessarily. At the start of the twenty-first century, Britain's caesarean section rate was just below 22 per cent. Latest data (2006) puts it at around 24.8 per cent.[1] Assuming an optimal rate of around 12 per cent, this means that around 55,000 women a year are having unnecessary operations.

Three studies undertaken in 1991–2, 1996 and 2004 showed that mothers' low emotional wellbeing and negative feelings about their babies were both associated with having had a caesarean.[2] The risk of endometritis, need for transfusion and pneumonia are higher following a caesarean compared to spontaneous vaginal birth.[3] One study of the post-operative health issues associated with caesarean section found that only 9.5 per cent of women had no recorded health problem in the postnatal period and concluded that there were considerable postnatal health issues associated with the operation, particularly if it is carried out as an emergency procedure.[4] This was also the finding in our recent survey of women's experiences.[5]

Literature on effects of caesarean birth on the infant is limited and there appears to be little research on the long-term effects of caesarean birth on child development. The evidence available does not suggest increased use of caesareans to have reduced infant illness or death and there may be problems for the baby associated with not having gone through the rigours of labour and risk of respiratory disorders in caesarean-born infants.[6] In view of the wealth of evidence pointing to negative side effects of caesarean section for the mother, and to a certain extent the infant, it is not unreasonable to assume that these effects will have repercussions on the mother–child relationship. Caesarean mothers have reported negative effects on bonding[7,8,9] and breastfeeding.[10,11,12,13,14]

We believe that the caesarean rate in the United Kingdom is too high and that too many caesareans are being performed unnecessarily. Our aim is to encourage women and their partners to question recommendations for caesareans in cases where they may not be necessary and may not be the best course of action.

When we asked consultant obstetricians and midwives why they believed the caesarean rate was rising, 68 per cent of obstetricians and 51 per cent of the midwives said that one of the reasons was maternal request, demand, pressure, or expectation. In addition, 62.5 per cent of midwives and 55 per cent of obstetricians said that another reason the rate is rising is because of fear of litigation and the practice of defensive obstetrics.[15] What this means is that according to health care professionals, the caesarean section rate is rising not because of medical reasons or the physical condition of women, but because of non-medical considerations. Obviously such considerations are not recorded on women's medical notes. When we spoke to women about why they had caesareans, none mentioned litigation and very few said that they had requested the operation.[16] When a caesarean is suggested to you, you will be told it is because of medical necessity and/or safety for you and/or your baby.

There are some reasons (indications is the word used in medical practice) for which a caesarean section is always needed – the absolute indications. In the majority of operations there is an element of judgement or discretion and this is why individual obstetricians may have very different caesarean section rates despite having similar populations of women or working in the same hospital.

In this handbook we examine each of the reasons you may be given for having a caesarean; review any evidence on the relative advantages and disadvantages for caesarean birth in those circumstances; and draw on medical and other expert opinion as well as lay experiences, so that you can develop an informed opinion as to whether or not a caesarean is the best option for you. The middle section of the book covers choices for care and how these may help you to avoid unnecessary caesareans. The final section is compiled from five birth stories from women who were told during their pregnancies that they would need a caesarean; but who, by arming themselves with information and constructive support, managed to avoid unnecessary caesareans.

At the beginning of the twentieth century, the main reasons for women having their first caesareans were:

- Problems with the baby (presumed fetal compromise) – 28 per cent
- Labour taking too long (dystocia or failure to progress) – 25 per cent
- Breech presentation – 14 per cent.

For women having subsequent caesareans, the main reasons were:

- Previous caesarean – 44 per cent
- Maternal request (as reported by doctors) – 12 per cent
- Labour taking too long (dystocia or failure to progress) – 10 per cent
- Problems with the baby (presumed fetal compromise) – 9 per cent – and breech presentation.[17]

Overall, over 85 per cent of caesareans were carried out for one of four main reasons:

- Repeat caesareans – 29 per cent
- Fetal distress – 22 per cent
- Failure to progress (dystocia) – 20 per cent
- Breech presentation – 16 per cent.[18]

We discuss each of these and other reasons below:

Repeat caesareans

Repeat caesareans account for a considerable proportion of all caesareans. As the number of women having caesareans for their first baby rises, an inevitable increase in the number of repeat caesareans follows, despite a wealth of evidence showing vaginal birth after caesarean (VBAC) to be a viable and preferable alternative to repeat caesareans.[19]

The practice of repeat caesareans began in the early 1900s when the rationale behind it had a logical medical basis. At that time the vertical cut in the body of the uterus (classical) predominated and such scars were prone to rupture particularly during the rigours of labour because the upper part of the uterus is very muscular. The lower-segment transverse uterine incision (the bikini-line cut) in general use today is much less vulnerable to rupture and is associated with lower incidence of maternal and fetal health risks and complications and death. Indeed discussions of uterine rupture are misleading as it is rare. What usually happens is that the scar gives way (dehiscence is the medical term) or comes 'unzipped'. There is only a little bleeding and it does not usually result in any serious problems for mother or baby if recognised early and swift action is taken to deliver the baby.

Over 20 years ago the World Health Organisation (WHO) stated:

There is no evidence that caesarean section is required after a previous transverse low-segment caesarean section birth.[20]

In the year 2000, 67 per cent of women with previous sections had repeat caesareans.[21] One way to stem the increasing tide of repeat caesareans is firstly to reduce the number of primary caesareans being performed and secondly, to increase the proportion of women having VBAC (see our handbook *Vaginal Birth after Caesarean* for more information on VBAC[22]). As the number of caesareans increases, the success rate of VBAC after two caesareans rises, and this practice should be encouraged in suitable women.

Risks from repeat caesareans
Routine repeat caesarean section is associated with higher risks of complications and more potential problems than VBAC[23] and offers no advantage to you or your baby.

Some of the complications associated with repeat caesareans are:

- Bladder injury at time of repeat caesarean[24,25]
- Increased risk of bleeding (haemorrhage)
- Blood transfusions and fever after the birth are more common in women who have repeat caesareans[26]
- Increased risk of emergency hysterectomy – one study put the risk of emergency hysterectomy at one in 90 for women with one previous caesarean having a repeat operation[27]
- Some women may become clinically 'shocked' after surgery, usually because of blood loss
- Thromboembolism – this is where clots in the veins cause blockage (or partial blockage) in the blood stream following surgery
- Higher health risks for the baby[28] – two recent US papers suggest that more babies died after caesareans done without a medical reason[29,30]
- Repeat caesareans may increase risk of maternal death.[31]

Caesareans have always been associated with slightly higher maternal death rates, although the extent to which this is due to the condition for which the caesarean was performed or to the operation itself is unclear. In the UK between 2000 and 2002 the fatality rate for vaginal birth was 48 per 100,000 maternities, considerably less than for caesarean section at 172 per 100,000.[32]

Reasons you may be given for a caesarean

Problems with the baby: presumed fetal compromise/fetal distress

This is now the leading cause of primary caesareans. In general, fetal distress means that the baby is showing evidence of suffering from lack of oxygen (asphyxia). The commonest signs are that the baby becomes tired and moves less or it passes the contents of its bowels into the amniotic fluid. These are called 'soft' signs and do not require immediate action, but warrant watchfulness for other signs of fetal distress. These may be changes in the fetal heart rate as recorded by a monitor fixed over your abdomen or a clip attached to the baby's head. This information about the fetal heart rate is fed into a machine called a cardiotocograph or CTG for short. The process is referred to as electronic fetal monitoring or EFM.

You are more likely to labour successfully and thereby avoid emergency caesarean if you are not continually monitored in this way during labour. This is because EFM restricts your mobility as you are strapped to a machine and often required to lie on a bed. If you cannot move around as you please your labour may not progress or you may experience more discomfort which can affect your perception of the progress of your labour.

Also, if you are lying on your back your blood pressure may fall because your uterus may press on the large vein that brings blood back to your heart. About three to six per cent of women may suffer from this problem which is known as supine hypotension when it is severe. If your blood pressure falls it may affect your baby's heart rate and be seen as a sign of fetal distress.

EFM is sometimes poorly understood or the results can be misread and for this reason it is associated with higher rates of caesarean section. If your attendants want to check your baby with EFM ask them to take their readings and then remove the straps that attach you to the machine so that you can move. Continuous monitoring is recommended by the Royal College of Obstetricians and Gynaecologists but is not mandatory and is not recommended by their US counterparts in the American College of Obstetricians and Gynecologists. Research shows that intermittent monitoring every five minutes is just as effective.[33,34]

Labour taking too long (failure to progress/dystocia)

This term is used to describe a variety of different classifications of labours considered to be not 'normal'. Most commonly the term relates to complications regarding the length of labour but can be extended to include other problems occurring during the process of labour itself. In a woman having her first baby, the cervix usually dilates at 1cm per hour once she is in active labour which fits with the mean length of labour of 12 hours (although the range can be between 6 and 24 hours in the majority of women). In some cases failure to progress can be treated by the administration of drugs such as oxytocin to increase the strength of contractions and may prevent the need for a caesarean. However, the rate at which oxytocin is used for this condition varies from 47 to 100 per cent in UK hospitals.

Whilst we do not advocate that women be left to labour for days, there is debate amongst obstetricians and midwives regarding just how long is too long. In 1970 O'Driscoll and his colleagues at the National Maternity Hospital in Dublin reported a trial in which they took 12 hours as the limit for a first labour and actively managed women whose labours were going slowly by artificially rupturing the membranes and using oxytocin.[35] They showed that they reduced the caesarean rate without detriment to the babies and this approach was enthusiastically taken up in both the UK and the USA.

Subsequent work found variable success rates[36] and the National Institute for Clinical Excellence (NICE) guidelines state that 'active management of labour and early amniotomy have not been shown to influence the likelihood of caesarean section for failure to progress and should not be offered for this reason'.[37]

As long as your baby is ok, you do not feel exhausted and there is progress (albeit slower than the average), you do not necessarily have to accept advice about strengthening the contractions. Sometimes getting into a warm bath, walking around and having something to eat or drink may help. Also sometimes the cervix may not be dilating but there may be other signs of progress, for example the cervix may be effacing or the baby's head might be rotating, flexing or descending in the birth canal, so it is worth asking whether any of these signs of progress can be detected. These subtle changes of progress are best evaluated if the same person is doing the vaginal examinations as there may be differences in how midwives and doctors estimate cervical dilation.

- *Occipito-posterior (OP) position as a cause of failure to progress*
In about 6 per cent of women the baby is lying with its back against its mother's back instead of her tummy wall so that the back of the head is next to her spine and the face looks towards the pubic bone in the front of the pelvis. In the normal position with a head-first (or vertex) presentation the baby's occiput (the back part of the head) is towards the pubic bone and the baby faces the base of the mother's spine.

OP is not always easy to diagnose, particularly in larger women, as feeling the baby through the abdomen is more difficult. If your midwife listens to the fetal heart and it is on the opposite side from where she/he thinks the back of the baby is lying that may alert her before she does the vaginal examination.

With the OP position the baby's head has to rotate more as it descends in the pelvis and this takes longer. With an OP baby the dilatation may be only 1cm in two hours instead of the usual 1cm per hour, but as long as progress is steady, the baby in good condition and the head is descending and rotation is occurring there is no need for the health care professionals to speed up your labour. You may experience more pain with this type of presentation and here an epidural may transform your experience. The neck of your baby may be more extended than usual so that there is a bigger diameter of the baby's head coming down through your pelvis and sometimes at full dilatation the head becomes stuck. If this happens the midwife or obstetrician may help the baby out with the vacuum extractor, fingers or forceps to flex the head and complete the rotation, so that the baby can be delivered in the usual way.

If your baby is found to be in the OP position you may try exercises advocated by some midwives to help reposition the baby. However, in general you will need to be ready for a longer labour. You may want to discuss pain relief and the use of oxytocin if progress is very slow.

- *Where there is not enough room for the baby to pass through the pelvis (cephalopelvic disproportion (CPD) or fetopelvic disproportion) as a cause of failure to progress*

What this means is that the woman's pelvis is too small for the baby's head to pass through. Although absolute or severe disproportion was common in this country in the nineteenth century because of poor nutrition leading to rickets affecting the growth of the pelvis and is still common in developing countries like Africa, this is uncommon in the UK today.

CPD can rarely be diagnosed before labour begins and almost never in a woman having her first baby. Today fractured pelvises from road accidents are the commonest cause though still relatively rare.

It used to be the case that, where CPD was suspected, attempts were made to assess the size of the baby using clinical palpation (feeling through the abdomen), X-rays and/or ultrasound. Recent studies have shown that such attempts to assess whether or not the baby can pass through the pelvis are unreliable predictors: some women whose pelvises have been shown to be radiologically inadequate have succeeded in giving birth vaginally; and some women whose pelvises have been shown to be radiologically adequate have required emergency caesareans; so the Royal College of Obstetricians and Gynaecologists (RCOG) does not recommend this.[38]

If your consultant has ordered X-rays of your pelvis, these can be used as an aid to discussions about the management of a vaginal birth. Talking though the tangible evidence of the X-ray picture of the bones of the pelvis with your consultant and midwives may help you to labour more confidently.

The increase in caesareans due to failure to progress does not seem likely to have been due to an increase in small or abnormal pelvises as women today are taller and generally have had better nutrition in childhood than their mothers. The proportion of large babies has not increased compared with a 1958 survey when the caesarean section rate was 2.8 per cent. Attitudes about the length of labour and how rapidly it should progress may have changed and it is possible that women are less fit than they used to be. However, it again seems intrinsically unlikely that so many women really need a caesarean for this reason – unless it has something to do with our modern system for delivering women in large units with a variety of often unknown people looking after them, which may affect the way that women labour.

Breech presentation

Breech presentation means that the baby is positioned bottom down (frank breech) or feet down (footling breech) at the time leading to delivery, instead of the usual position of head first (vertex presentation). The proportion of babies who present as a breech has remained static at around 3 to 4 per cent. Statistics for the 1980s in Britain show that about 40 per cent of breech presentations were delivered by caesarean; by the 1990s this number reached a staggering 72 per cent of breech presentations in one health authority region of this country.[39]

One woman who told us about her experiences said:

> My first c-section with my first child was for breech presentation. My son was diagnosed breech at 36 weeks and they told me they could try and turn him or I could have an elective c-section. I asked if turning him would be safe and the doctor said it would be very painful, it might not work, my baby could turn back again or the placenta could come away and I would need an immediate caesarean. I was scared by this and even though I didn't want a caesarean I agreed to an elective. I went into labour five days before the elective was booked so they told me they were going to give me a section right away. It was a very traumatic experience and one that I didn't want to repeat!

There has been debate for many years about the best way to deliver a baby presenting bottom first instead of head first. Comparisons of the safety of vaginal versus caesarean birth for babies presenting as breech are complicated because babies are more likely to be breech earlier in the pregnancy and premature babies are more likely to die. Also some babies with congenital anomalies are more likely to present by the breech and more likely to die. Thus it is not necessarily breech presentation per se that causes these deaths.

Small-scale randomised controlled trials (RCTs) did not show convincing evidence that caesarean was preferable for the baby; and of course, the mother has the additional problems that follow any surgical operation.[40] The 'term breech trial' was a large RCT with participants from many countries.[41] Many obstetricians think that this has been the definitive answer that the profession and women have been looking for and this is certainly the view of the NICE guideline group. They recommended that planned caesareans should be offered to women with a term singleton breech presentation, and so you may hear reference to this 'trial' if your baby is in breech.

However, there are some obstetricians, and many midwives, who are not convinced by this study. Roosmalen and Roosmalen pointed out that several of the 13 perinatal deaths in the planned vaginal group were not related to breech delivery. One was cephalic (head first) and so the death could not have been due to breech presentation or delivery; and one was a stillborn twin, that should not have been in the trial at all as the study was of singletons.[42]

A report from Shrewsbury in 2005 of 1,400 term breech babies over a ten-year period showed that 38 per cent were delivered by planned caesarean, just over 32 per cent had a caesarean in labour and 29 per cent had a vaginal breech birth. The overall infant death rate was 2.8 per thousand. There was one death of a baby directly attributable to breech delivery.[43]

Women faced with a breech presentation at term may be offered external cephalic version (ECV) where the doctor attempts to turn the baby round to a head-first position using manual pressure. Like everything in life this procedure is not completely without risk and for some years in the seventies and eighties its use fell out of fashion. There may be transient fetal heart changes in up to 16 per cent of pregnancies and 3 per cent will be admitted for induction of labour. One per cent will have painless vaginal bleeding and in a similar number there will be some separation of the placenta according to a systematic review by Hofmeyer.[44] In an attempt to reduce the caesarean section rate, the Royal College of Obstetricians and Gynaecologists (RCOG) issued a guideline in 1999 recommending that all women should be offered ECV.[45]

In the National Audit of Caesarean Birth (2000) a third of women who had a caesarean had been offered ECV but there is no data about how many women had a successful version. A systematic review in 2001 concluded that there was significant reduction in breech births and caesarean section in women who had had an ECV compared with those who had not.[46]

The difficulty for women is that younger obstetricians have often little or no experience in breech delivery and so in effect it is safer to have a planned caesarean than a badly managed vaginal breech birth. However, it is not difficult to learn the skills needed and the Advanced Life Support Obstetrics (ALSO) course has trained over one thousand midwives, GPs and obstetricians since its inception (see www.also.org.uk).

The important thing with a breech birth is to let the baby descend on its own through the birth canal and not pull the body down. Patience is the answer and in the past obstetricians were taught to 'sit on their hands'. Once the head enters the pelvis, the blood supply to the baby is cut off and it is essential to look at the clock because the minutes seem like hours as the baby often makes attempts to breathe whilst the body is hanging down. It may be useful at this stage for you to adopt the upright or kneeling position. This seems to help the natural process of birth and is certainly preferable to the 'stranded beetle' or lithotomy position (where the woman lies on her back with her legs supported by stirrups) favoured by conventional obstetrics.

Benna Waites, when faced with a breech presentation, was shocked by how little information was available to women. After researching the area she published a very useful and readable book reviewing the literature and dealing with her emotional reactions which we are sure you will find helpful.[47] The Association for Improvements in Maternity Services (AIMS) has produced a breech edition of its newsletter with an article by Mary Cronk, a midwife with immense experience in breech birth, which gives some useful advice.[48]

You will see from the birth stories at the end of this book that three of the women who gave their stories to us were advised to have caesareans for breech presentations. All three declined and successfully achieved vaginal birth, one feet first and two bottom first (see pages 57–74).

Where the baby is not presenting head first or moves position (malpresentations and unstable lie)

There are some types of presentation where it is recommended that a caesarean be performed and others where this may not always be necessary. The key is to get as much information about the position of your baby as you can and discuss options for birth with your obstetrician and midwives.

The normal way for the baby to lie in the womb is with the head flexed so that the vertex, a point on the skull between the two soft areas (the

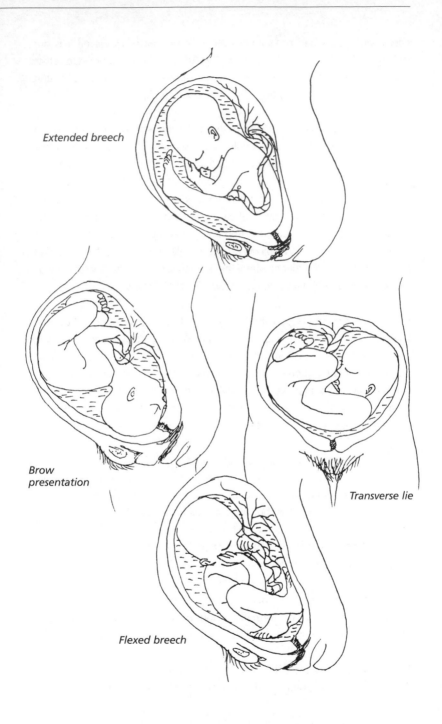

Extended breech

Brow
presentation

Transverse lie

Flexed breech

fontanelles), is the lowest point of the head. This means that the smallest diameter of the head will be passing down the bony pelvis as the head is well flexed. If the head is extended, either the face or the brow is leading. When the brow or forehead is the leading part of the head of a term baby the diameter is too large to go through the average pelvis and a caesarean is inevitable. With a face presentation if the chin is at the front (mento-anterior) the head can be born if it flexes but if the baby's position is with the chin at the back of the pelvis the back of the head gets stuck above the pubic bone and a caesarean is needed.

Normally the baby lies with its spine parallel to that of the mother's body and womb; but if the baby lies across the womb (transverse lie) or is oblique (lying with its head or bottom under the ribs on the left or right and the other end of the baby near the bone above the hip) or swinging around from one position to another, there is a risk of cord prolapse (see page 24) when the woman goes into labour.

- *Transverse lie*
With a transverse lie a scan will show whether there is a low-lying placenta, fibroid or ovarian cyst preventing the head from entering the pelvis, which would indicate the need for a planned caesarean. If none of these conditions are present, it is possible to wait until labour begins to see if the baby will move or can be turned to the normal position. However, once the waters have broken with a transverse lie and the liquor drained away, the uterus clamps around the baby's body and a caesarean is needed.

- *Oblique lie*
Waiting for labour to start with an oblique lie may allow you to deliver naturally as the contractions often straighten up the position of your baby.

- *Unstable lie*
Unstable lie is more likely if you have had several children, so waiting in hospital until labour starts may be an unattractive option; but if you understand what to do when you feel contractions or the waters break, it is usually safe for you to remain at home. If your waters break before you are in labour your cervix is likely to be closed and, as your baby's head is not in your pelvis, in the unlikely event of a cord prolapse you can adopt the knee chest position to prevent pressure on the cord until you get to hospital. What

you will need to do is to get on all fours, and then move so that you support your body on your elbows and put your bottom up in the air with your knees below. This prevents the baby pressing on the cord and cutting off the blood supply in the cord. It will also help to keep the cord in the vagina where it is warm and so the blood vessels do not shrink up because of the cold air. Not elegant but life-saving for the baby.

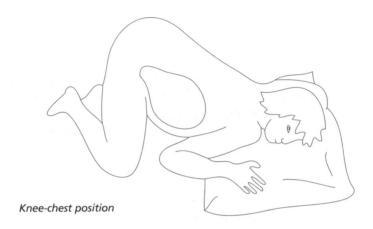

Knee-chest position

Problems with the placenta

Bleeding from the vagina during pregnancy should always be taken seriously and reported to a midwife or doctor; although in the majority of cases the bleeding stops and may be due to 'incidental causes', a polyp or cervical infection, or a cause that is never ascertained. There are two serious causes which may lead to caesarean section: placenta praevia and placental abruption. However, this depends on the severity of the condition and a caesarean can be avoided in certain circumstances.

• *Placenta praevia*
Placenta praevia is where the placenta is in the lower part of the uterus rather than the upper part. If the placenta completely covers the cervix or encroaches on it (grade 3 or 4) you will have to have a caesarean. If the placenta is less far down (grade 1 or 2) a vaginal delivery is possible. With the practice of routine ultrasound scanning many women are told they have a low-lying placenta at 18–20 weeks but in the majority of cases (90–95 per

cent) the placenta will be drawn away from the lower part of the uterus as this grows during the pregnancy. It is usual to repeat the scan at 32 weeks to see if that has happened. Another scan will be needed at 36 weeks if the placenta is still low at 32 weeks. Often there is no problem then.

- *Placental abruption or abruptio placentae*

In this condition the placenta separates from the wall of the uterus. If the separation is massive it can be fatal to the baby and you can become shocked by the pain and the blood loss. If you are in labour your membranes may be ruptured to facilitate vaginal birth but if the cervix is closed a caesarean will be carried out. Fortunately this is rare and, if the baby is alive, swift action to perform a caesarean will save the baby and allow you to receive treatment. This condition is more likely to occur if you have high blood pressure.

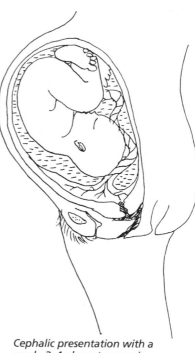

Cephalic presentation with a grade 3–4 placenta praevia

If there is only a small amount of bleeding, the pregnancy can continue to full term with careful checking of your baby's growth by your midwife to ensure that the placenta is transferring enough oxygen to the baby.

Eclampsia, pre-eclampsia (PET) and HELLP syndrome

- *High blood pressure*

High blood pressure can exist before pregnancy but more frequently develops during pregnancy. The cause of this is still unknown, but it may be caused by the placenta not developing properly in early pregnancy, thus raising the mother's blood pressure to compensate for the poor functioning of the placenta.[49] It usually develops after 24 weeks and, generally speaking, there are two types: an early onset, often rapidly progressing type between 28 and 34 weeks; and a late onset, fairly benign condition later on in the pregnancy. Delivery cures the condition so the objective is to allow the baby to grow and mature as long as possible whilst controlling the blood pressure so that the mother does not suffer ill effects.

- *Pre-eclampsia (PET)*
High blood pressure together with swelling and protein in the urine is known as PET or pregnancy related hypertension (PRH), or pregnancy induced hypertension, and is more common in first pregnancies and in African or Afro-Caribbean women. If the disease is progressing fast and induction of labour seems unlikely to succeed then a planned caesarean is usually performed. In the uncommon but life-threatening condition of eclampsia, when the woman has fits, a caesarean may be life saving for her and the baby.

- *HELLP*
In the HELLP syndrome (which seems to be increasing in incidence), platelet numbers decline (platelets are small blood cells which are important in making the blood clot) and there are changes in the way the liver functions. There may therefore be problems with blood clotting which are dangerous for the mother. Early delivery is advisable, so induction may be advised and if the condition is combined with PET this may mean caesarean section. However, you should discuss the pros and cons with your obstetrician.

Cord prolapse

Usually the head or bottom of the baby fits snugly into the brim of the pelvis so that, when the waters break, the cord remains in the fluid still in the upper part of the uterus. If however, the cervix is open then there is nothing to stop the cord from being washed down into the birth canal and coming out of the vagina. This is known as cord prolapse. Cord prolapse is a life-threatening condition for the baby and requires immediate caesarean section in a cephalic presentation, as the blood supply to the baby can be cut off as the head enters the pelvis. This occurred in about one in a thousand pregnancies in the past but the National Audit does not give exact figures for this.

Maternal age

Obstetric complications and interventions are more common in older women[50] due to diseases such as diabetes mellitus and pre-eclamptic toxaemia.[51] It is usually assumed that the higher rates of interventions experienced by these women are a consequence of the increased risks of childbirth as women age. Indeed, increased maternal age does appear to be associated with higher caesarean section rates and it has been suggested that the fact that many women are delaying childbirth until they are in their thirties or forties is a reason for increasing caesarean rates. Women under 30 years of age are choosing to both delay childbirth and have fewer children.[52] What this means is that older mothers constitute a larger proportion of all maternities. Only 6 per cent of mothers were over 35 years of age in 1975, by 1995 11 per cent were over 35[53] and in 2000 16 per cent of mothers were 35 or over.[54] By 2004 the birth rate among women in their early thirties had overtaken the rate for mothers in their late twenties, and in 2005 birth rates in women aged 40 and over were 50 per cent higher compared to 2000.[55]

There is a debate about whether older mothers require caesarean section more often but no conclusive evidence to suggest increased obstetric complications in older mothers necessitating the increased caesarean rates.[56,57] One study found that the correlation between higher maternal age and caesarean rates persisted even when obstetric complications were controlled for.[58] What is more, countries in Scandinavia have experienced similar demographic changes but have not encountered corresponding increases in caesarean rates.[59] The Scottish Health Department report suggests that clinicians may adopt different selection criteria for caesareans in older mothers and it is this that pushes up the caesarean rate for these women.[60] If you are an 'older' mother and a caesarean has been suggested to you, find out what the precise reasons are for this and make sure that the caesarean is necessary on medical grounds rather than perceived risk factors. If necessary you could ask for a second opinion or change obstetricians.

Multiple births

Twins account for about one in 80 births in the UK and the incidence of triplets is normally about one in 6,000. In 2001 only 1.49 per cent of deliveries were multiple births (1.45 per cent of births being twins, 0.04 per cent triplets or more).[61]

Many twins and most triplets are now born by caesarean and there is debate over the efficacy of this practice. Some researchers have suggested that it is safer for twins to be born by caesarean.[62] However, the use of caesarean section for multiple pregnancies has increased without good evidence of benefit.[63] Triplets, for example, can be delivered vaginally safely[64] yet only three sets achieved this in the National Audit in 2000, 92 per cent being delivered by caesarean. In 3.5 per cent of cases caesarean was done for the second twin after vaginal delivery of the first twin and this is a situation where internal version and breech extraction can be done if the second twin is not presenting as it should (where the doctor puts a hand into the uterus and moves the baby round to breech which can then be delivered vaginally) – again a skill that younger obstetricians may not be acquiring. Expecting that labour will progress normally to a vaginal birth even if the first twin is breech would be appreciated by many women. Emma Mahoney spoke movingly about how she had to fight to experience delivering twins normally at a meeting of the Forum of Maternity and the Newborn at the Royal Society of Medicine in 2004 and has written a delightful book about her experience.[65]

Quadruplets and higher-order births are usually born by caesarean, but the evidence of this practice is scant. The number of pregnancies resulting from in vitro fertilisation (IVF) treatment is affecting the number of multiple births. The Human Fertilisation and Embryology Authority have advised that the number of embryos implanted during IVF should be reduced from three to two. This would reduce the number of multiple births from IVF treatment but the number of twins may not be affected. However, caesarean rates for multiple births present a minor contribution to overall caesarean section rates.

Maternal medical disease
• *Diabetes*
Diabetes is probably the most important disease affecting pregnant women although far fewer women today have a planned caesarean for this cause now that diabetic control is much better. However the baby may be large and it may be considered that a planned caesarean is preferable to a long difficult labour.

• *Neurological conditions*
Certain rare neurological conditions do not allow the woman to push. For example, if a woman has had a stroke (due to a sub-arachnoid haemorrhage

for example) or has raised pressure inside the skull (as in hydrocephalus), a caesarean will be done.

- *Heart problems (cardiac disease)*

Many women with cardiac disease are safer having a vaginal delivery than a caesarean with the added problems of surgery and lengthy recovery period.

- *Previous vaginal surgery*

Sometimes women develop dropping of the uterus or vaginal wall outside the vagina. This is called prolapse and some women can be treated surgically which means there is scar tissue in the vagina. This operation is called a repair and, whilst usually done after menopause, can affect women of childbearing age. Another birth will cause the problem to recur. Women who have had a vaginal repair for prolapse are advised to have a planned caesarean so that the repair holds.

- *HIV*

Caesareans are often advised for HIV+ mothers as it reduces the risk of the baby acquiring the infection but surgery is of questionable benefit for the mother.

- *Herpes*

Primary herpes simplex in the last trimester of pregnancy is an indication for caesarean section, to reduce the risk of transmission of the virus to the baby. Recurrent herpes is not an indication for surgery as antibodies will have been transferred to the baby from the mother which protect the baby from infection.

Dealing with the system

Continuity of carer

The more comfortable you feel with the place of birth and the people caring for you, the more likely it is that your birth will be straightforward. Being looked after by people with whom you have a good relationship will empower you to make informed choices. Women who have one-to-one trained support during labour have lower caesarean section rates.[66] Women in labour appear to value the special relationship of trust that being with women entails and continuing support in labour may influence whether or not you have a caesarean.[67]

Increasingly, the emphasis in enlightened systems of maternity care aiming at the minimum number of medical interventions (and therefore only necessary caesareans) is on continuity of carer. Continuity of carer can be defined for these purposes as getting to know a small group of midwives responsible for your care during pregnancy, birth and postnatally. In particular, the midwife looking after you during labour should have got to know you during pregnancy and be able to care for you according to your preferences. Even if you need medical assistance, you can continue to receive much of your care from midwives. Some GPs offer the whole package of maternity care, including care during labour, to their patients, but usually rely on community midwives to give much of that care. However, you can often receive a high level of continuity from this kind of arrangement, quite different from the usual 'shared care' package.

Much modern maternity care is fragmented, with many women being cared for by a large number of different health professionals during pregnancy, birth and afterwards. Most midwives work in teams but the number in those teams can range from two to 16.[68]

Often nowadays the only way to achieve continuity of carer, particularly in urban areas, is to book a home birth or domino system (see Appendix A). In rural areas, particularly those served by small maternity units, continuity of carer is more likely to happen because there are smaller numbers of both women and midwives so it is easier for them to get to know each other. In a few areas, efforts are being made to improve continuity of carer as a result of the Royal College of Obstetrician and Gynaecologists Audit Report in 2001.

Choosing the type of maternity care

It is important that you are not rushed into arranging your care during pregnancy and birth until you have had time to find out all the options available and to consider which type of care is best for you. It is very common for a woman to visit her GP after a positive pregnancy test and be expected to decide on her care there and then. GPs are not always fully aware of the options for care available to women and therefore refer women directly to consultant units, restricting their choice.[69] Women from the same GP practice can be given different choices about treatment, screening and types of maternity care.[70]

Many women find it hard to access services without referral from a GP.[71] You can get more information about options for your care from the local branch of the National Childbirth Trust (NCT) (see Further information for parents, page 89), community midwives (usually based at the nearest maternity unit), community health councils (still available in some areas, check your telephone directory or the Internet), family and friends. There are a number of online organisations offering information and advice (see page 89 'Further information for parents') as well as NHS Direct (by telephone or on the Internet at www.nhsdirect.nhs.uk). The table in Appendix A shows the basic features of each type of maternity care. In addition to options provided by the NHS, some women may wish and be able to afford to use an independent midwife.

When looking into your local options, you can enquire about the approaches to care during pregnancy and birth and can also ask for up-to-date statistics as well as any other factors or facilities such as the availability of a birthing pool or special care baby unit. Caesarean rates can often be an indicator of a more-or-less technological approach to birth (we have published recent data on caesarean rates by hospital in Appendix B), but it is important to find out at the same time whether a unit with a substantially lower caesarean rate than another unit in the same health district is only caring for women at 'low risk' of complications during labour. Caesarean rates are often also linked to forceps and/or ventouse rates so that if one is lower, the other may be higher. If you have a pre-existing medical condition or a difficult obstetric history, it is probably wise to discuss the implications for pregnancy and birth with an obstetrician and/or other medical specialist before deciding on your care.

If you decide to give birth in hospital, you can arrange to visit and be given a guided tour. This will provide an idea of the atmosphere of the maternity unit and the opportunity to ask questions informally. Some units organise regular weekly tours for this purpose, often in relation to antenatal classes.

In addition to the choices of place of birth, midwives and style of care, another variable you will need to take into account when choosing your care is the approach and policies of individual consultant obstetricians. Their attitude to the management of labour can affect the chance of having a caesarean significantly. Informal sources of this information might include the senior midwife in charge of the hospital antenatal clinic and local branches of the NCT and AIMS (Association for Improvements in Maternity Services). Other more direct sources would be the senior manager of maternity services or the clinical director. These data are collected and processed at the taxpayer's expense and should therefore be available to the public. Care should be taken in interpreting data as some consultants may specialise in high-risk cases. GPs may be able to help.

Once you have found out about all the local options for care and any special implications arising for you, you can consider which type of care feels right. If you have a partner, you may want to take his or her views into account, especially if she/he is going to be with you in labour. Alternatively, if your partner's attitudes to the place of birth differ to yours, or if you prefer, you can ask a friend or relative to be your labour companion.

Home versus hospital birth

The 1994 study of home births compared low-risk women who had booked for home birth with those booked for hospital birth. The home birth group had fewer interventions in labour, and although some were transferred because of slow progress in labour, the caesarean section and assisted vaginal birth rate was half that of those booked for hospital birth. The outcome for the babies was similar and the NICE guidelines for caesarean section state that healthy women with an anticipated normal pregnancy should be told that their risk of having a caesarean is halved if they book for home birth.[72]

Even if you do have to transfer to hospital, the further along you are in your labour when you enter hospital, the more likely you are to have a vaginal birth. It is also recorded that in hospital one type of intervention leads to another and often culminates in caesarean section.[73] Thus by planning a home birth, you can retain a degree of control over what happens to you and labour in as natural way as possible.

The home birth study suggested that there is something about the hospital environment that affects the chances of a woman delivering normally.[74] It is likely that labour wards with their bright lights, telephones ringing, bleeps going off and frequent interruptions do militate against successful labour. Some women can be affected by being in hospital (white coat syndrome) which makes them more anxious and therefore affects the progress of labour. This can lead to the labour being diagnosed as taking too long (dystocia or failure to progress) which can ultimately lead to caesarean section. Women need peace and quiet, with as few professionals as possible involved, and privacy. In addition, the sound of other women labouring is not conducive to relaxation and the state of inner concentration that women need to deliver normally.

What this means is that your choice of where to give birth is a personal one and one that you will have to make once you have collected all the relevant information about your pregnancy and the support you will need.

Choosing a home birth

In many ways, having a baby at home is the surest way of achieving continuity of carer, avoiding routine procedures and intervention, encouraging the normal progress of labour and thus minimising the risk of a caesarean. However, since childbirth in Britain has become medicalised, many women do not have confidence in their ability to give birth without medical supervision and therefore feel more secure labouring in hospital. We acknowledge this need and therefore welcome the trend to make hospitals more homely and welcoming to women, their labour companions and families.

If you are thinking of giving birth at home, you can discuss this with your GP, a community midwife, an independent midwife, the NCT or a local home birth support group (the local NCT branch should have details). Some GPs are very supportive of home birth and will attend women in labour at home or provide 'cover' for community midwives. Some GPs are opposed to home birth,[75] and unfortunately have been known to strike off their lists women and their families for requesting a home birth, although this is against government policy.[76] If you are unable to arrange a home birth through your GP, you can contact the local community midwives direct or telephone or write to the Director of Maternity Services or the Supervisor of Midwives (sometimes these are the same person) requesting a home birth. The Supervisor of Midwives has a legal duty to arrange midwifery care for a woman she knows is pregnant, and this must be provided at home if that is what the women wishes. If a GP goes so far as to strike you off his/her list for requesting a home birth, you can complain in writing to the local Family Health Services Appeal Authority (address in telephone directory or on the Internet at www.fhsaa.org.uk).

Many women who go ahead and book a home birth with community midwives are asked to go and see a consultant obstetrician in hospital. In most cases, this is more or less a courtesy visit, giving you and your obstetrician the opportunity to meet and to discuss the emergency back-up available from the hospital and the circumstances in which transfer to hospital might be advisable. In other cases, the appointment is used by the obstetrician to try to dissuade women from giving birth at home by 'shroud waving' and other unfair means. If or when you are invited to meet an obstetrician you can usually discover from discreet enquiries what form the consultation is likely to take and can accept or decline the invitation accordingly. You do not have to go if you do not wish to. It is generally accepted that you should have at least one medical examination during your pregnancy to check your heart and lungs, but this can usually be done by your GP if you prefer.

Getting support from NHS midwives
Home births are usually attended by community midwives. To book a home birth you will need to contact the Head of Midwifery or Supervisor of Midwives at your local hospital. You do not need the support of your GP, in fact you do not have to discuss it with your GP unless you want to, although

it may be politic to let her or him know your plans.

Women in the UK have a right to home birth but it appears that there is no obligation on the part of the primary care trusts (PCTs) to provide obstetric care at home. Some PCTs may be unsupportive of home birth because of the perceived 'risks', but armed with information and knowledge about the safety of vaginal birth you should be able to negotiate appropriate care. (See the home birth website for more information and advice on www.homebirth.org.uk/homebirthuk.htm.)

In a recent statement on home birth from the Nursing and Midwifery Council, the Chief Executive, Sarah Thewlis, stated:

> ...all midwives have a responsibility to ensure that all women receive care that is based on partnership with women and respects the individuality of a woman and her family. Women have the right to make their own decisions on these issues if they are competent to do so and midwives have a duty of care to respect a woman's choice.[77]

Where a midwife does not feel confident to attend a home birth, it is unacceptable for her to refuse a home birth and take no further action. Rather, the midwifery guidelines state that she must take steps to update her knowledge and experience to ensure her confidence with home birth in the future and, importantly, refer you on to another midwife who does have the confidence to attend a home birth.

Employing an independent midwife

Independent midwives (IMs) are fully trained and qualified midwives who have chosen to work outside of the NHS and are self-employed. As such they can be engaged by individuals to work with and for them. The going rate for an IM is from about £1,800 to £4,500 (approximately) for the whole package of care. You are still entitled to NHS treatment and services such as blood tests and scans if you employ an IM.

The IM's role is to care for you during pregnancy, birth and afterwards. They can work with you whether you are planning a home birth or a hospital birth. If you start labour at home and transfer to hospital they can accompany you as your birth partner or supporter but would be unable to give clinical care once in hospital except in a tiny minority of cases so your clinical care would transfer to NHS staff at this stage.

The advantage of having an IM is that you can choose your midwife and be assured of continuity of care. IMs are supportive of women's choices and many take on the care of women who are deemed 'high risk' including those who have had previous caesareans. They give you advice and information to empower you to make informed decisions about the birth of your baby. They will be there to support you during labour and act as your advocate in terms of ensuring your wishes are considered at times when you may not be able to assert yourself.

Private versus NHS facilities

You are more likely to have a caesarean if you opt to give birth in private health facilities than if you use the NHS. In the UK as in other countries, caesarean rates are higher in private facilities than they are in publicly provided health care. For example, the Portland Hospital in London (private) has a caesarean section rate of 50 per cent[78] whereas the highest rates in NHS hospitals are around 30 per cent.[79]

Birth plans

At some point during your antenatal care, perhaps during the last two or three months of your pregnancy, you should discuss with your midwife your preferences for labour. These discussions could include how long you want to stay at home in labour before going into hospital and what sort of pain relief you may prefer. People vary and some women write a birth plan setting out exactly what they would like to happen at every stage of their labour. Others prefer to wait and see what happens, choosing to make their decisions at the time, or are content to take the advice of the midwives and doctors looking after them during labour. The latter may be a satisfactory approach if your view of birth is the same as that of your caregivers, but if the hospital's approach is very 'high-tech' and you would prefer a 'low-tech' approach, for example, you may have a disappointing experience. Also, if you have strong feelings about what you would or would not like from your care, these may get lost if they are not written down.

Currently some people have doubts about the value of birth plans. Some health professionals have been scathing about what they perceive as unrealistic, aggressively phrased birth plans insisting on no intervention, whose authors have ended up experiencing a large number of interventions, often after a change of heart. Some hospitals have short-circuited the system by producing their own form of birth plan with check-lists which may or may not correspond with an individual woman's agenda, only to ignore the plan when a woman goes into labour.

You should feel able to write a birth plan if you want to but need not feel obliged to do so. In any case you should discuss the sort of care you would like during labour with your midwife antenatally. You could ask your partner or other labour companion to attend the appointment with you so that they are able to be present at the discussion and understand the hospital's approach to the management of labour. Alternatively (this tends to happen when a woman receives care from a small team of midwives or from an independent midwife) you may prefer to discuss different aspects of labour at different times during your pregnancy as your knowledge of what to expect and ideas about your own preferences develop. Another approach is for you and your partner each to write your own birth plans and then to compare notes.

A formal birth plan that you have written can set the agenda for discussion with your midwife. An alternative approach is for you to ask about hospital policies regarding the areas of concern to you and to focus in your birth plan on those issues where your preferences differ from hospital policy. For example, there may be a policy that every woman in labour has her waters broken by the midwife at 3cm dilatation or on admission into hospital, whichever is the earlier. In these circumstances, you might ask that your waters be left to break spontaneously on the grounds that research shows that there is no benefit in breaking them early on in a normal labour. When adopting this approach, if you find that your preferences differ from hospital policy in only a few aspects, you could ask the midwife to record your preferences in your notes, rather than write a formal birth plan or fill in a checklist. If you do write a birth plan, it is advisable for it to be tactfully phrased and to take account of any professional advice about the possibilities for your birth.

Information on how to develop a birth plan and what to include is now available online – see for example: www.babycentre.co.uk. You can even fill in a birth plan online at www.amazingpregnancy.com.

With a view to avoiding an unnecessary caesarean, if you are experiencing a normal pregnancy and anticipating a normal labour you might consider some of the following aspects of care:

- If you are found to be in the latent phase of labour when you go into hospital, find out whether you can return home until the contractions become stronger. You will be more relaxed at home whereas in hospital you may become anxious and staff may feel they have to 'do something' if you have a long latent phase.
- Whether there is a policy for listening to the baby's heartbeat using continuous electronic fetal heart monitoring, in both normal and abnormal labour. In our 2005 survey 11 per cent of consultants said they did monitor all women electronically and half also did a short admission trace despite the RCOG guidelines which do not advise an admission trace. It might be easier to discuss this with the Head of Midwifery who should be involved in formulating departmental protocols to see if this could be changed.
- Whether fetal blood sampling is used to check if abnormalities in the recording of the baby's heart rate are noted. The evidence is that this reduces the need for caesarean section and if this is not available then you might consider transferring to another hospital where it is done.
- Whether the waters are routinely broken artificially (and if so, when) or whether they are allowed to break spontaneously. Again, use the evidence to ask why this is done and ensure your wishes are recorded in your notes.
- Whether you can eat and drink if you are hungry and thirsty throughout labour. There is no reason why you should not be allowed to eat and drink during labour (see page 43). If necessary, change hospitals.
- Whether you can take up whichever position you feel most comfortable in at every stage of labour, even if your baby's heart is being monitored. Research from the 1950s showed that the upright position increases the strength of contractions. If there are rigid rules against freedom of movement we suggest you change hospitals or opt for a home birth.
- Whether any time limits are set for the first and second stages of labour. Women and labour vary and as long as you and your baby are well and labour is progressing then intervention on these grounds is unnecessary.

If there are rigid rules laid down it may be a warning sign that intervention rates are high so change hospitals.

- How the onset of the active phase of labour is defined – for example, when the cervix is 3cm dilated, fully effaced and you are experiencing strong regular contractions. Intervention when you are not in established labour can start a spiral of treatment: artificial rupture of the membranes and/or oxytocin to induce labour leads to more painful contractions, then an epidural because the pain is worse which can reduce the urge to push leading to prolonged labour and ultimately caesarean section.
- In what circumstances an oxytocin drip is used to accelerate labour. This is a matter of judgement and not usually used routinely. But if there is a rule that labour must be accelerated if progress is less than 1cm an hour in women having their first babies then beware.
- Whether, in the latent phase of the second stage of labour, you will be allowed to wait until you have an urge to push. Not all women experience this but again if you and your baby are fine arbitrary time limits are unhelpful.

If you are experiencing any complications you might in addition ask about the following:

- What effect, if any, a pre-existing medical condition or disability might have on the management of your labour
- What effect a pregnancy-related illness such as gestational diabetes, raised blood pressure or pre-eclampsia might have on the management of your labour
- Whether external cephalic version is attempted to turn breech babies and if so, when
- The management of a breech labour
- The management of a multiple births
- The availability of epidural or spinal anaesthesia for a planned or emergency caesarean
- Whether your labour companion can be present during all procedures.

If you have written a formal birth plan, once the final form has been agreed you should prepare two copies – one for yourself and one to be kept with your notes – both of which should be signed by you and your midwife or obstetrician. In some hospitals, a woman wishing to use a birth plan is asked to see a doctor. If this is the case, you should insist that the doctor is not a trainee with less than three years' experience but either your consultant or a senior member of his or her team whose participation in the process of negotiating the birth plan will be meaningful.

Choosing between a planned caesarean and a planned labour

If you are faced with one of the relative indications for caesarean such as suspected fetopelvic disproportion, you may be given a choice between a planned caesarean and labour. You will obviously discuss your choice with your obstetrician. Although the obstetrician is likely to advise you to take one course or the other, you should feel able to choose which feels right for you and, if necessary, to ask for a second opinion from another obstetrician. You should obtain as much information as there is about your obstetric condition, including the chances of giving birth vaginally. You should also ask whether an epidural or spinal anaesthetic will be available to you for a planned or emergency caesarean.

Some women prefer the certainty of preparing for a planned caesarean – hopefully under regional anaesthesia, knowing the date on which their baby will be born and being able to make all necessary preparations – to the uncertainty of waiting for labour to begin spontaneously and then perhaps ending up with a caesarean, possibly under general anaesthetic. However, obstetricians are unlikely to offer a planned caesarean unless there is a medical reason for it. Other women prefer to give their bodies every chance to give birth unaided and, if an emergency caesarean is necessary, derive satisfaction from the knowledge that they tried everything they could to avoid a caesarean. However, most women who have no need for a caesarean would prefer not to have one.[80]

It is vital that if you are presented with such a choice you think carefully about your decision. You may find it helpful to discuss the matter with your midwife, partner or with a woman who has gone through a similar experience (NCT branches keep 'experiences registers' and some run caesarean support groups) as well as your obstetrician. You can then make an informed choice based on what is right for you.

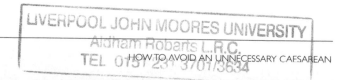

HOW TO AVOID AN UNNECESSARY CAESAREAN

Increasing your chances of a normal labour

Ways in which you can be helped to deliver vaginally are as follows:

- Declining induction of labour for non-urgent reasons if the cervix is unripe.

- Staying at home as long as possible. You may find that using a TENS (transcutaneous electrical nerve stimulation) machine or warm bath for pain relief at home enables you to delay going into hospital.

- Having a home assessment in labour from community midwives is usually possible on a domino or team midwifery scheme. You may find it reassuring to be given a vaginal examination to see how far your cervix has dilated and to have the baby's heart rate checked.

- If a home assessment in labour is not possible, you may find it reassuring to keep in touch by telephone with midwives on the hospital labour ward who will tell you whether it is advisable to remain at home.

- Being looked after by midwives you have got to know antenatally and who know you and your preferences.

- Procedures or interventions should not be carried out for routine reasons, but because they are necessary in your labour. All procedures and interventions should be explained fully to you, together with the reasons for performing them.

- Not being continuously connected to an electronic fetal heart rate monitor unless there is some doubt about the baby's condition. Research shows that listening to the baby's heart rate at regular intervals is just as effective. What matters is that any doubtful results should be considered carefully and any necessary action taken quickly.

- Doubtful traces from the electronic fetal heart rate monitor should be checked using fetal blood sampling for further evidence of the baby's condition.

- Not having your waters broken artificially unless there is a good reason for doing so. Routine policy is an inadequate reason.

- Not having your labour accelerated using an oxytocin drip unless there is a good reason for doing so, since some babies become distressed as a result of their oxygen supply being reduced by the artificially strengthened contractions. Conforming to arbitrary time limits is an inadequate reason for acceleration.

- Careful use of epidurals for routine pain relief. Your contractions may become weaker as a result of reduced mobility and you may then be given an oxytocin drip to strengthen the contractions, which may adversely affect the baby. Sometimes a woman embarking on labour is recommended to have an epidural so that she can be awake in the event of an emergency caesarean becoming necessary. However, managing labour in this way could make a caesarean a self-fulfilling prophecy. You might be much more likely to deliver vaginally if you are able to use self-help techniques such as adopting an upright position and moving around to promote the natural progress of labour and to maximise the ability of your pelvis to expand to accommodate the baby.

- Being as relaxed as possible, both during and between contractions, so as not to interfere with the natural process of labour.

- You are likely to find upright positions the most comfortable and these use gravity to aid the process of labour.

- Using a breathing technique for coping with contractions learned antenatally. One technique is to concentrate on the out-breath, letting the breaths in take care of themselves. This ensures that you, your baby and the uterus have enough oxygen to cope with the hard work of labour.

- Remaining mobile and changing position. Different positions will feel comfortable at different times in labour. If you listen to your body you can automatically take up the position most useful for labour. If the baby is in an awkward position, walking around, pelvic rocking and other rhythmic movements may help it to turn into the right position.

- Touch and massage. Good for contractions experienced as back pain and for helping you feel less isolated during contractions. If you find that you do not want to be touched or held in labour, you should make this known to those with you!

- Darkness promotes the release of endorphins, the body's natural painkillers produced in response to pain. Another way of helping you to concentrate on yourself and your labour if you wear glasses or contact lenses is to remove them. But you may prefer to keep them on and may also appreciate eye contact to help you stay with your contractions

- Food and drink. Essential during a long labour since a labouring woman uses 700–1,000 calories per hour. Many hospitals do not allow even women at low risk of complications to eat or drink during the active phase of labour on the grounds that they may inhale acid stomach contents during a general anaesthetic. However, research shows that it is usually faulty anaesthetic technique and insufficiently experienced operators which cause this to happen. Possible ways round such a policy are to put unrestricted eating and drinking in a birth plan, to stay at home as long as possible and to eat and drink right up to the end of the latent phase of labour. However, do eat easily digestible food.

- Using large cushions, bean bags, birthing chairs, music and so on to get as comfortable as possible. A labour companion is good to lean on too!

- Using a birthing pool or warm bath can be an effective form of pain relief and may help you to stay relaxed, particularly if you use long baths as a way of coping with everyday life. However, the use of water for pain relief in labour has not been scientifically evaluated.

- Natural therapies such as homeopathy, acupuncture, hypnotherapy and aromatherapy can be useful in labour if you use them in normal life and if you know a practitioner who will attend you in labour. The advantage of hypnotherapy is that you can be taught self-hypnosis for labour so that the practitioner does not have to be on call. Some homeopaths suggest a kit of remedies useful for labour and can instruct you (and your labour companion) when to use them in labour or suggest remedies over the telephone. Supporters of natural therapies believe that they can promote the normal progress of labour and thus keep interventions to a minimum.

Birth stories

Many of the reasons why a caesarean is recommended arise during labour and, as such, are difficult to predict. We have included five birth stories in this section of the book, all from women who were advised to have caesareans because of conditions present during pregnancy. Two had previous caesareans and three had babies presenting in breech when the caesareans were recommended, two bottom first, one feet first. All resisted pressure from health care professionals in order to achieve the vaginal births they wanted. The stories are personal accounts, mostly of positive experiences but also some difficult ones. We hope that sharing these women's emotions and experiences will give you information, hope and determination in avoiding an unnecessary caesarean when it is not the right option for you.

STORY ONE

Two vaginal births in hospital after two caesareans

After a caesarean for her first baby, Kate had wanted a vaginal birth for her second child but was not supported in this by her health care professionals. During her third pregnancy Kate researched the viability of vaginal birth after caesarean (VBAC) and found some supportive health professionals. Despite placental abruption in her first VBAC, Kate went on to have a second successful VBAC completely naturally.

VBAC babies Josephine and Charlie with their caesarean siblings Isabel and Olivia

Kate's two vaginal births after two caesareans – Olivia, Isabel, Charlie and Josephine

On 3 June 2000 we found out that our first IVF (in vitro fertilisation) cycle had failed, and I was devastated. One month later, nature had done her stuff and after a week's denial I did the test that changed my life and saw that blue line! The first thing I did was to enquire about NCT classes: as far as I was concerned it was part of the rite of passage that was pregnancy. My husband and I started the classes after Christmas 2001. I was so excited and, having read every book possible, I knew all the technical terms. We duly went and sat with the other eight expectant parents each Wednesday evening for two hours. Sadly, I was concentrating more on my baby's hiccups than really listening to our teacher and ended up with a section without so much as a twinge, let alone a contraction. I was convinced I would not come home with a live baby and so, when the consultant suggested a caesarean after two failed induction attempts well before my due date (I had a condition called 'polyhydramnios' – too much amniotic fluid), I jumped at the chance. I didn't care how the baby was born, I just wanted a baby! I do not agree with what happened but at the time there was every chance that this would be our only child and I was just desperate to see it. When I hobbled through the front door five days later I felt let down that I hadn't 'given birth'.

When I was pregnant with number two I knew that I wanted to try and give birth naturally and naively thought that the medical profession would help me achieve that. I couldn't have been more wrong. I went into hospital at pretty much the first twinge and was strapped to a monitor. The registrar who attended to me was extremely fierce and, dare I say, aggressive. She certainly wouldn't 'let' me get off the bed and, in my uninformed state, I didn't realise that I could do what I wanted. Isabel was born by caesarean after nine hours of labour having been told I had to be permanently monitored and couldn't move. 'Like a lamb to the slaughter' springs to mind.

My second child was a 'colicky' baby. In hindsight, I am not sure if that is because she picked up on my feelings or that she really wasn't happy in herself, but by the time she was six months old I was on antidepressants, suffering from postnatal depression caused entirely (in my view) by the completely unnecessary section. When she was 11 months old I discovered that I was pregnant for the third time. I had spent pretty much all of Isabel's life researching VBACs so I knew that this time there was no reason that I couldn't do it. I also knew that I HAD to have a vaginal birth. It mattered to me (and still does) that I wasn't going to be cut open again.

Twelve months later I was sitting in my doctor's surgery listening to him saying that both my unborn baby and I would die if I attempted a VBA2C. He was wrong! I surfed the Internet daily for any information and statistics that would further my cause. I was determined to birth my own baby. We arranged to attend an NCT day course. I actually paid some attention and came out of there empowered. I knew that my body could do it, I just had to find some health professionals who would support me. We decided at 30 weeks to try a different hospital, where we met my consultant who agreed with us, encouraging me to have a water birth if I wanted. Charlie was born after a labour lasting one hour, culminating in a placental abruption and an episiotomy. I walked out of hospital with my husband 12 hours after Charlie was born – an impossibility after a section.

Ten months later I was pregnant with our fourth baby. I was keen on a home birth this time, especially as Charlie had arrived so quickly. Again we were referred to the hospital where I had my VBAC, mainly to see the consultant and discuss the possibility of another abruption. I was slightly more at risk but not dangerously so – I had a 0.1 per cent chance of uterine rupture and a 4 per cent chance of abruption. Our plans were full steam ahead for the HBA2C. Again we booked in for a two-day NCT course. I wanted to cover all options so that if I ended up with another section, it wasn't because I wasn't prepared for the birth. Towards the end of the pregnancy the baby couldn't make up its mind which way round it wanted to be, going from head down to breech to transverse. My consultant said that even I couldn't give birth to a sideways baby, although he was happy to support me birthing a breech one. We got a bit nervous so it was agreed that I would go and stay in hospital around the time we thought the baby would arrive. Charlie (my previous VBAC baby) was 11 days late, so I felt (and the consultant agreed) that this one wouldn't make an appearance any earlier, although I lived in hope. I ended up being admitted 14 days overdue when things looked as though they might kick off at any moment.

Three days later I was still in hospital having had a very lazy weekend. I began to have a few twinges around lunchtime on the Monday. By the early evening the twinges had become regular and it was obvious that something was going to happen that evening. My husband Philip arrived at 6.45pm and apart from a midwife trying to tell him he wasn't allowed on the ward (I told him and her that he was) things were going ok. I was using the TENS machine by now, which was great and enabled me to carry on watching the Commonwealth Games without too much bother. After about half an hour, I decided that I wanted to go over to the labour ward as the gas and air was beginning to sound appealing. However, when I went to the loo I realised that the baby was on its way. I panicked slightly and, screaming for Philip, I pulled the emergency cord (always wanted to do that). Philip and a midwife burst in (fortunately I had forgotten to lock the door) and bundled me into a wheelchair with a cot sheet covering my modesty!

So our fourth child and third daughter was born after an official labour of one hour with a further five minutes of pushing. She was our only completely natural birth and was the largest (a whopping 10lb 12oz or 4.86kg). I gave birth half kneeling, half squatting. She was born at 8.15pm, and at five to midnight the three of us left the hospital. What an amazing way to complete our family – four is plenty for us.

Charlie (number three) was very much my 'cure' and I am very proud of my achievement of both VBA2Cs which my husband and I fought so hard to get. It saddens me that, even now, people are amazed to hear that I was 'allowed' to have a natural delivery and also that I have had to spend some of my last two pregnancies fighting to get the birth that I was cheated out of with Isabel and to a smaller extent Olivia (number one).

I am horrified when so-called celebrities say how much easier a section is compared to natural birth. I do understand that sometimes there is a genuine need for a section but in my view it is not the easy option. If I had my time again I would never have agreed so readily to that first one.

STORY TWO

A vaginal birth at home in a birthing pool after two caesareans

Taryn achieved a successful VBAC at home after a traumatic labour and emergency caesarean with her first child followed by a planned caesarean for her second based on misinformation, despite the fact that she had wanted a vaginal birth.

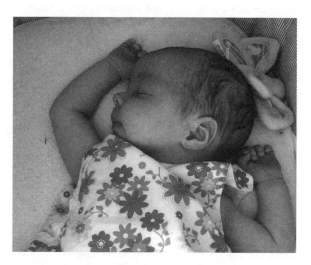

Taryn's VBAC baby Tegan at two weeks old

Taryn's HBA2C story – Tegan

We knew we wanted a third and final baby (final as we know three caesarean sections is meant to be the limit), but I could not face the thought of another caesarean section. When I fell pregnant, and went to my first appointment with my community midwife, she had already put me down for a caesarean section without asking, and was prepared to book a date at that appointment. This time I had access to the Internet from home, and a chance remark from a neighbour asking why I couldn't have it naturally, instead of being told I shouldn't, led me to do some research into the possibility of a home birth.

Then started the gradual process of further research, and sitting down and discussing it with my husband. As soon as I told him of the outcomes of various studies, and the much lower risks than we had been led to believe, and that in fact the size of the baby didn't matter as we had been told in my previous pregnancy, we decided to start preparing to have a home birth. After a lot of discussion we decided that an independent midwife was the way to go, and would try and raise the cash from somewhere. No matter what was said in guidelines, saying we should be supported in whatever our decision for birth was, we knew it would be a struggle to get what we wanted, and would always be on the hospital/midwife's terms rather than a more relaxed approach. I seriously could not face hospital again, and knew that even if by some miracle they let me book a home birth, on the day they would rush me into hospital at the slightest hint of a problem. This was pressure I knew I couldn't take. I knew I needed a more relaxed, less clinical atmosphere if I was going to succeed. If anything was to prove this, at my 20-week appointment the registrar (it was meant to be a consultant!) already assumed I was having a caesarean section. When I said I wanted a VBAC, she said ok, but she didn't recommend it, I would probably fail, and gave me about a 40 per cent success rate, when in reality studies have shown it to be nearer 65–70 per cent. She then booked me in for a growth scan nearer the birth, which we knew I didn't need, and was just a way to get us back in and be pressurised into having a caesarean section. Later, when the independent midwife wrote to the consultant to say she was taking over the care, he sent back quite a sarcastic letter, and cancelled the scan without consulting us. We didn't want the scan anyway, but it really annoyed our midwife, as we should have been consulted first.

We emailed a few midwives, including the Bristol Birth Practice. The first midwife we met was lovely, but we didn't feel completely right with her. Another midwife we chose from the Bristol Birth Practice website was fully booked, but she recommended another. We met them both, and from that minute all the earlier stresses just disappeared. We immediately felt that we had found the right midwife for us, and after they left we were even more determined to find the money.

The pregnancy went well, and the antenatal appointments were a joy. It was amazing having someone come to your house and spend a huge amount of time with you, compared with a community midwife. With all the research we continued doing and all the books our midwife lent us, I was able to work through all the issues of my previous births, and give myself the confidence that my body was not a failure, and that I could give birth naturally. It was an amazing feeling, and my confidence in myself started returning. I had put on a lot of weight, and was very depressed after my first two children. I put on a brave face, just happy that I had my two wonderful boys, but deep inside I felt such a failure. I had already lost the weight to get ready for this pregnancy, and now finally I was starting to feel mentally prepared as well.

We bought our 'Birth Pool in a Box' and enjoyed the rest of the pregnancy, eager for the baby to arrive. For the final few weeks I was having strong Braxton Hicks in the evenings and it became a game of 'will tonight be the night?' Just after my due date, my husband and second son went down with a really bad stomach bug, and we were praying that the birth wouldn't start, as my husband was in no fit state to help, or come in the birth pool with me. I got into bed that night with strong Braxton Hicks, and about an hour later had to get up to go to the toilet. Although I had finished weeing, fluid was still coming out and so I thought might waters might have gone. I fetched a pad, and settled in bed not really believing anything could happen – although I did whisper to my husband that I thought my waters had broken, and we were both really excited, especially as the contractions started to get stronger, and closer, but with no real pattern to them. It was too uncomfortable to sleep, so I got up, baked cakes, and filled the pool between contractions. My husband was also running up to the loo to be ill, and running to my youngest son to help him.

We phoned our family at 4am to come and look after our two sons, and phoned our midwife in the morning. Unfortunately, when she arrived my contractions had died off, so I just relaxed in the pool as I was so tired. As we were unsure as to what was going on, we all decided that it would be a good idea if the midwife gave me an internal. The outcome was that I was still in the very early stages. Our midwife decided it would be best if she left us alone to relax, and came back once labour had started again, which could be anything from hours away to several days.

We tried to sleep during the day, but my contractions kept disturbing me every 20 minutes or so. We went to bed at 9pm, but a horrendously painful contraction woke me at 11pm, and we went back downstairs. From then until about 5am I kept having really painful contractions without any pattern, but which seemed to occur whenever I moved position. I then had an incredible need to get in the birth pool, but my husband who had napped for a couple of hours while my mum looked after me, insisted on phoning the midwife first. Unfortunately he was still a bit drowsy, and didn't realise how things had changed since he went to sleep, and that I had progressed quite a bit. As far as he could tell my contractions were still not regular, but were coming stronger, and more often than before.

I got in the birthing pool, and the contractions accelerated, whilst my husband phoned the midwife back and told her to get over as quickly as possible. It was now just after 8am. Having recovered from his stomach bug, my husband jumped in the pool to help me through the contractions, which had become incredibly painful. Despite several requests from me to take me to hospital, my husband helped me calm down, and we worked through each contraction. My sister was also watching, and I think I scared them both at one point, when I said 'If the midwife doesn't get here I trust you both to help me deliver the baby.' Within no time at all I decided to do my own internal exam, which is something I said I would never want to do, and I felt the head. I told my husband to do the same. It is one of the most incredible things I have ever felt.

At this point my contractions started to change, and my body totally took over. I started to have more time between contractions, my body started to bear down, and I started grunting with each contraction. Shortly after, at 9.30am, our midwife arrived. I started to feel the head coming down, and then moving back up. This is something I had never felt before, and was nothing like I had expected it to be. I was shocked at how well I could feel it, and even asked the midwife if it was normal (I felt so stupid). A second midwife arrived at 10.10am and was quickly briefed on the situation. I then had one huge contraction that I couldn't control, and I felt myself tear, and the head came out. I shouted that this had happened, but I don't think anyone believed it for a couple of seconds, as it happened so quickly. I then said that the head was in my hand, and everyone rushed around to get towels, etc. The rest of the baby was delivered with the next contraction, and the midwife passed her through my legs at 10.16am and onto my chest, where we rubbed her with towels, and made sure her breathing was ok. It was such a relaxed atmosphere, we almost forgot to check to see what sex the baby was. I suggested we had a look, and my husband checked. It was a girl, we couldn't believe it, we even double checked!!! We left the cord pulsing, and she latched on for her first feed. We stayed this way for 20 minutes, whilst we introduced her to our children, and my parents. They then left me to concentrate on delivering the placenta. We decided to get out of the pool, to check how much I had torn, and also investigate where I was bleeding from, as the water was quite dark at this point. Unfortunately as my legs were quite weak, we decided to cut the cord before the placenta arrived, to help me get out of the pool. My husband was extremely happy to finally be able to cut the cord, as he hadn't been able to do it for either of our boys.

Once I had climbed out of the pool, I lay down in some blankets, and fed our daughter while I was checked over. I had two tears, neither of which needed stitches. The placenta was taking a long time to come out, and the midwives were concerned about a pocket of blood behind some tissue so we decided to have the injection to speed up the delivery of the placenta, which was delivered shortly after. The pocket of tissue turned out to be part of the placenta, and not a haematoma.

As a celebratory meal my husband went and got some fresh bread, and a selection of soft cheeses that we had bought ready. It felt like one of the best meals I have ever had in my life. The usual checks were done, and we found out that she was only slightly lighter than either of the boys, at 8lb 11.5oz. At about 12.30 my husband took the baby, whilst the midwife helped me into a nice warm bath. After that we went to bed for the rest of the day. Although I was in pain with the tears, my recovery rate has been amazing compared to either of the caesarean sections, and my energy levels have been a lot higher. When I look back I realise how tired and depressed I was after both my boys. It took me months to recover after them. My daughter has been a much more content baby, and hardly cries – in fact, she has only ever woken for a feed once or twice during the night. More importantly, she came out without any kind of bruising, and has never seemed to be in pain.

We are so glad we went for a home birth, because my waters broke so early that the hospital would never have let me wait so long. That would have meant a third caesarean section. My birth was wonderful and relaxed, and I got to get into my own bed with my husband and baby, without a horrid hospital stay. I also feel as if I could have more children in the future without the fear of a caesarean section hanging over my head. I would never say no to one if it was definitely needed and the baby was in any trouble; but neither would I have one just because the labour was not progressing at the rate a hospital would want. If I have any more children I will be saving for an independent midwife again.

STORY THREE

A bottom-first breech birth in hospital

Melanie originally wanted a home water birth. By 32 weeks it became apparent that her baby was in breech and she was told that she would have to have a caesarean. She transferred to a different consultant and successfully achieved a vaginal breech birth at 38 weeks.

Melanie and Finn

Melanie's breech baby – Finn

I am a vegetarian who eats organically and utilises alternative medicine. I have researched and lectured on women's reproductive rights for several years. Throughout my pregnancy I felt very happy and healthy (though I had some spotting at 13 weeks). I decided from early on that I would like a home birth with a birthing pool. I read lots of books about pregnancy and birth and asked for advice from friends. At 24 weeks I therefore decided to contact an independent midwife, Judith.

I always felt a fluttering, then tapping feeling inside, and the baby flipped about several times a day as if his arms were moving. At 32 weeks, though, the baby was quite firmly settled with his head under my ribcage and his tapping feet above my pubic bone. I discussed with Judith that this might be a breech baby and she gave me lots of literature on it. My mother told me that her first baby, my sister, had been breech. My sister's first was also breech.

At 36 weeks the baby was big and healthy and still settled in the breech position. Judith told me that she wouldn't advise a home birth now unless it turned. With her help I therefore tried homeopathy, moxibustion (an oriental medicine therapy utilizing moxa, or mugwort herb), and walking around on all fours. I also went with Judith and my husband to discuss my options with the consultant at the hospital I had booked into. Judith warned me that the consultant might try to force me to have a caesarean, but that I was entitled to transfer to a different consultant at a different hospital if I wanted, where I might be allowed to attempt to have a natural breech birth. As predicted, the first consultant told me that I would have to book in for an elective caesarean. She seemed actually relieved when I told her of my intention to transfer to somebody else, and sanctioned this. This new consultant at St. Mary's hospital, Manchester, (a University Teaching Hospital) was in favour of natural breech births being attempted, though mine would be a rare occurrence even there.

I accepted the new consultant's offer of an external cephalic version at 37/38 weeks. I had a scan at 36 weeks and 37 weeks to see if my baby was still in a breech position. On a Friday afternoon in late January I had the ECV. The consultant made two or three attempts to turn the baby manually, but the baby did not budge. I tried to relax but it was the most painful thing I had ever had done. (I also regret the ECV now as it is not advisable if you are Rhesus negative as it can cause miscarriage of subsequent pregnancies. At the time though, my only thought was to avoid a caesarean.) When the ECV failed, the consultant told me there was now a 50 per cent chance that I would have to have a caesarean.

Two days later, on the Sunday afternoon, my back began to ache. By 9.30pm I told my husband the pain was coming rhythmically, like contractions, every six minutes. I rang Judith at 11pm. She came over to the house and examined me – I was 2–3cm dilated. The contractions weren't painful and I breathed deeply through them. She went home at 12am, told me to wait as long as possible before going to hospital, but to ring her whenever I wanted to. I tried to relax in bed but eventually thought I wasn't going to be able to travel in the car if I waited much longer.

We rang Judith at 3.30am and she said she would meet us outside the hospital. I travelled in the back of the car on all fours, with Greg pointing out the signposts on the way to keep me calm. We met Judith who took me to a delivery room and I happily got into bed under the blankets. We were then joined by a young consultant who I hadn't met before. He criticised my apparent idea of having a normal delivery. He told me he was the senior obstetrician on duty and would decide what happened because my consultant was not there (which is why Judith had told me to wait as long as possible before going to the hospital!) To make matters worse he told me that the hospital could not find my notes authorising a normal delivery. He asked me whether I had read the latest research findings of the dangers of breech delivery versus caesarean. He showed no respect for me and little for Judith (who has many, many years experience). This while I was having contractions all the time! He then examined me and disputed that I was 3cm dilated (only 1cm he said) and told me to go home.

Luckily a nurse walked in with my notes. He left the room. Then Judith left and returned with great news about the team coming on duty at 8.30am. She advised me that I only had to keep going till then to show that the labour was progressing well and there was no need for a caesarean. So I got through the night trying different positions on the bed when I had a contraction. By 11.30am the contractions seemed non-stop and very painful.

As I thought there was still a 50:50 chance I still might have a caesarean I asked for an epidural. I told Judith that there was a small area through from my back to my left ovary where I could still feel the contractions. So I was topped up with Phentenol (a strong pain-killer). My husband and I then dozed for the next few hours. All this time I was attached to a heart rate monitor. The baby's heartbeat would disappear when I had a contraction and when the node would fall off me as I moved around with each contraction. I chose to largely ignore the machine, though, with it just beeping in the background.

At 5pm Judith examined me and said I was ready to start pushing as I was fully dilated and she could see the baby's bottom. Judith had experience of breech births and told us that the best thing for the midwife was to watch and wait. Judith then changed the bed shape so that two padded arms stuck out for me to lean my feet on as I pushed, and she elevated the top half of the bed so that I was in a semi-recumbent sitting position. Judith told me that every time I felt a contraction coming (which I luckily could still feel in the left ovary area) to try pushing from the abdomen down through my bottom as hard as I could, have a break, then do it again, and again. I could feel the baby coming down the birth canal. I reached down through my legs and could feel the baby's bottom all soft and warm. The first time I had felt my baby's skin. Greg and Judith kept encouraging me, then the baby's legs came out, then his torso. I leant forward and felt that too. It felt amazing.

Another midwife and a woman consultant were now watching closely. I tried to push out the head but couldn't. The consultant said to Judith, 'I'm afraid I'm going to have to do an episiotomy.' She then quickly did one, inserted forceps and quickly but gently pulled the head out. He had the cord wrapped around his neck and she un-looped the cord. The second midwife took the baby over to the paediatrician who gave him oxygen. The baby then seemed to become more lively. They washed him then handed him to Greg while I was being stitched up. He was quietly elated, but I must admit I felt exhausted and very emotional. I then held him and tried to feed him while Judith took a photo. She asked us if he had a name and we both said, 'Finn, of course!' We both felt really happy and relaxed. Judith washed me and we told her to go home as she looked so tired. I was wheeled up to the private en-suite room I'd booked and enjoyed some tea and toast. I tried to feed him again, then lay him on the bed and lay down next to him staring at him all night totally besotted. After breakfast in bed I put Finn in his cot and showered and got ready. I was allowed home that afternoon.

So Finn came two weeks early at 6lb. He was long but skinny. He took to breastfeeding and always had a big appetite. Now he is six years old and still long, but not so skinny! I am very glad I had the opportunity to try a normal birth and am very grateful to all the staff at St. Mary's hospital who enabled that. I am particularly grateful to Judith as I know I couldn't have done it without her presence, care and learned advice. It's a shame that independent midwives are necessary, but until the value of all midwives is more greatly appreciated by all those involved in childbirth, they will remain the assets they are. I sincerely hope that future training in birth will include breech deliveries to the benefit of all concerned.

STORY FOUR

A bottom-first breech birth in hospital in New Zealand

Susan's baby was not discovered to be in breech until she was in labour. Under pressure to have a caesarean at that point, Susan felt that her body took control and started to do what it needed to do. She delivered her breech baby into the arms of her midwife whilst standing in a room full of onlookers.

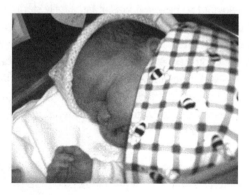

Joseph

Susan's breech baby – Joseph

Two weeks or more of false alarms and I had just about started thinking the baby would never actually arrive. At almost 42 weeks Karene (midwife extraordinaire) gave me some homeopathy (blue cohosh), and did a sweep to see if things were starting. She also commented that my tummy felt different when she 'palped' it, the baby obviously moving into a better position. He (and I'll just say we now know he is a he) would have lots of very quiet times too, but would quickly wake up if I had a cold drink, and it was so hot I was eating ice by the bucket-load. In retrospect it is no wonder that made him active – who wouldn't be with a glass of iced water being tipped on their head!

The other curious thing is that the previous Sunday night he was particularly active and we got it on video – I will always wonder now if in fact we captured 'the turn'!

On Saturday the 11th, not long after writing my last diary note, the contractions were getting quite intense and I had an instinctive feeling that today was the day. So Nana and Grandad collected our daughter Niamh about lunchtime and, you guessed it, all stopped. Later in the evening I sent my husband Seamus out for fish and chips and a 'swift pint' and of course, the minute the car went down the driveway it was all on, the minute he returned, all stopped. I went to bed quite early though as I was sure it was going to be tonight, and sure enough, was woken at 10.30pm by very strong contractions. Reluctant to believe it was at last finally starting, I kept moving around and trying to 'stay calm', even going so far as to get out of my pyjamas and get dressed. After an hour or so of timing the contractions, I rang Karene, timed the contractions again for another hour and she came round. By this time I was well ready to go to Matariki (small maternity unit, the next best thing to a homebirth), finding my back very painful and the contractions just manageable. Got to Matariki and laboured on the bed for a while before going in the pool.

The next few (seven) hours are a bit of a blur – I remember things getting tougher, not feeling there was an end in sight and needing lots of pressure on my back. I remember my waters breaking but that not helping the baby move and I ended up using gas, which took the edge off but didn't really do much else. I was quite upset about this as I had been so determined for a drug-free birth (not that gas is really a drug at all) and remember being quite teary about it. Quite early Sunday morning Karene got me out of the pool. It just wasn't providing the comfort I had hoped for anyway, mainly because it wasn't really big enough for me to stretch out in, and my really painful feet meant I couldn't bend my knees and ankles very well. After some discussion it was agreed that I would go to Waikato Hospital in an ambulance. I think that was the worst part of the whole experience – I don't recommend labour on all fours in a moving vehicle! At one point I said, 'Oh we're only at Ohaupo' (about half way in the 20 km journey). Then feeling blood pounding in my ears and blissful relief as I passed out. The next I remember was Karene saying, we're here at the hospital. For some reason I assumed I would be in A & E and was quite surprised to discover I was in the delivery suite. I also remember having a comical vision of me flying through the ward, on all fours with bum in the air for the entire world to see, although I am assured that I was covered modestly and this didn't actually happen!

I was whisked into a room and an ultrasound was done. 'That's not a head that's buttocks' I heard the surgeon say. Oh, action stations from the hospital staff! I was in a complete daze, mainly from the pain (the entire tank of gas I had used hadn't done a thing) and it was suggested I have a caesarean. I think I would have agreed to anything, but at that moment I blissed out again from the pain. (I later learnt that in fact I had stopped breathing and started having convulsions.) A frightening time for everyone, including Karene! I came to and found myself on my back, a room full of people and being told I needed a caesarean RIGHT NOW by general anaesthetic.

By this stage I would have agreed to anything so signed the papers but argued the point that I wanted a spinal block. I at least wanted to be awake for the birth of my baby. The surgeon and Karene stepped out to discuss next steps (it was to happen immediately) and a staff midwife said to the house surgeon 'Why is she having a caesarean, who's it for, the woman or you?' Very brave of her! The anaesthetist was telling me they wanted me to have a general anaesthetic and I was resisting.

In the space of a couple of minutes it was as if my body decided it needed to get into action – I was saying 'the baby's coming' and felt him move very quickly in my pelvis. All rushed back and sure enough he was right there! A mild sense of panic in the room and the surgeon instructs that I'm to have a lithotomy. I was coherent enough to ask what she meant and when told that it meant putting me in stirrups I completely freaked! That was the limit for me – I had an oxygen mask on which I ripped off (Karene said later that I looked furious) and shouted 'no! I'm not doing that.' So Karene looked at me and calmly said, 'ok, the best chance for your baby is for you to stand up, take the gas off and deliver him right now.' The fact that there was a room full of people suddenly became irrelevant as every bit of me focused on getting the baby born. Suddenly it seemed doable and close and I was totally empowered again – I had really felt like I was losing control, thinking about surgery and my birth plan and how everything seemed to be going against my wishes – and that I really could do what I had to do with the help of my awesome team of Seamus, Karene and Kelly (who had arrived unbeknown to me a few minutes earlier).

So, I stood up and said, 'ok, does anyone actually know how to deliver a breech baby?' – and there was complete silence in the room, apart from Karene who said 'of course I do.' The rest of the people seemed to fade into the background and we got on with it, me pushing like there was no tomorrow, Karene holding the baby as he emerged and Seamus standing on the other side of the bed holding my hands and looking, it must be said, a bit shell-shocked!

At the time, the effort seemed almost insurmountable, but I seemed to draw on a huge amount of inner strength, could feel the people around me willing me on, and felt my body respond to simply getting on with it. I had to listen carefully to Karene in order to deliver him safely (at one point I had a thought that I was very glad I wasn't at the receiving end – what a view!) but that really it wasn't any more difficult than Niamh's birth three years ago. Only a few pushes and he was out, bum first and then arms and legs falling down into Karene's hands. His head took only a couple of pushes and there he was! It seemed in fact, to be a relatively gentle birth considering there was a crowd in the room, bright lights and no pool – simply women getting on with what had to be done. Seamus holding my hands as tight as I would let him (although he told me later that the look on my face was scary and that I looked like my eyes were going to pop!) Within about 10 minutes my beautiful baby boy was born, whisked away for a few seconds to be checked and then handed back to me and yes it's true, I immediately forgot the pain and inconvenience of it all and was in love again!

All the extras in the room disappeared – it felt like I had quite an audience but can't remember when they actually left, and at last we were left in peace to meet Joseph. There was a fleeting moment when I realised I had actually had a baby but wasn't holding him, another moment of seeing what appeared to be blood everywhere (turned out the cord had not been clamped properly by the over-eager house surgeon) and then pure elation as Joseph was brought to us, warm and pink and healthy.

Unfortunately it turned out that my placenta got stuck – three hours of trying and everything short of hugging a tree and I ended up having to go to surgery to have it removed with a spinal block which left me unable to walk for a few hours. But by 2.00pm Niamh was up at the hospital to see her new brother and me and that was just brilliant. How ironic that I could deliver a 10lb 6oz baby, breech, with no drugs – but couldn't get that measly little placenta out! I was delighted to learn I had only a small first-degree tear and was told approvingly by the house surgeon I had a very 'accommodating pelvis!'

I spent the night at Waikato Hospital and then transferred to Matariki the next day. I'd lost nearly a litre of blood so was very light-headed but apart from that – perfect!

I thought I might feel cheated and disappointed that I didn't get my textbook Michel Odent water birth, but in fact all I felt, literally from the moment we went ahead with the delivery proper, was a complete sense of empowerment, strength and an amazing sense of calm. I have experienced something very, very few women get to do, with an amazing positive outcome. How could I be disappointed with that?'

STORY FIVE

A feet-first breech birth in hospital

When her second child was found to be lying in breech position, Ruth was told that a caesarean was her only option of delivery. She had hoped to have a home birth and did not want to have what she considered unnecessary surgery. Ruth tried every technique and therapy she learned to get her baby to turn, but the baby was determined to stay head up. Ruth was convinced that she could give birth to her baby naturally and found an NHS midwife and consultant who were not only happy to support her choice but applauded her decision to do so.

Ruth with Ruby

Ruth's 'upside down baby' – Ruby

At 33 weeks pregnant, my midwife confirmed what I had suspected – that my baby was in a breech position. I was told that if she remained breech, I would not be able to have the home birth I wanted and that a caesarean would be my only option.

With building renovation works in the house, and an active toddler, along with my dislike of hospitals and unnecessary medical intervention, I wanted to do everything within my power to help this baby turn around. The research into complementary techniques for turning breech babies began. I was prepared to give anything a go.

Things to try at home include: crawling around on all fours; positive visualisation; lying on your back, with your bottom elevated above your hips; putting headphones around the bottom of the bump, and shining a torch in the same area, to get the baby to turn towards the sound and/or light. All these and more were tried, but to no avail. A Chinese herbal remedy recommended Moxa sticks (Moxibustion), and when I lit one, the room filled with pungent smoke. I could hear the builders upstairs, wondering what drugs I might be smoking! This made her very active, but she did not turn. I was ready to enlist the help of various practitioners. I tried acupuncture, reflexology, osteopathy, chiropractic, craniosacral therapy and hypnotism. None of them worked. I was becoming increasingly anxious and broke.

My last hope rested on an external cephalic version to be carried out at the hospital. This resulted in having the baby rather roughly manipulated externally, with one hand on the baby's head and one on its bottom, trying to turn it. She would not budge. She was determined to stay exactly where she was, with her head firmly tucked up under my rib cage. When this did not work, I became very upset and got worse when I was told to make a date for a caesarean. I asked the midwife about the possibility of having a natural breech birth, or at least waiting to go into spontaneous labour, to give the baby every chance to turn, and to let her tell me when she was ready to come out. I was told that the chances of being allowed to have a natural breech birth were remote, unless I hired a private midwife. Everyone kept quoting the adverse findings from the 'term breech trial', but no-one could give me details of what these were.

My childrearing techniques are instinctive, doing what feels right to me – long-term breastfeeding, baby-weaning, bed-sharing and mother–baby togetherness. I believed in my body's power to give birth to my baby – I just needed to find someone else to believe in me, too. I knew that my much-desired homebirth was no longer a possibility, but I hoped I could still have a natural birth. More research was needed, and someone recommended a book by Benna Waite – *Breech Birth*. No local bookshops had it in stock, so I ordered it from the publishers.

Before the book arrived, I had an antenatal appointment with my midwife who informed me that I had created quite an impression at the hospital, with my refusal to book a date for a caesarean. Apparently, most people do what the consultants recommend, unquestioningly. She told me that if I had thought the whole thing through, that the hospital would let me try for a natural birth. This was very welcome news.

Caesareans have become so routine, that people seem to forget it is major abdominal surgery. Of course, they are essential occasionally, and have saved the lives of countless mothers and babies. I just did not want to sign up to one, when I believed that my body would be capable of doing what it was designed to do – give birth to my baby.

Benna Waite's book was exactly what I needed. I found it to be well written and researched. I was at last able to read about the term breech trial, and understand that the decision to opt for a natural delivery was not necessarily as onerous or irresponsible as the consultants had led me to believe. Her findings showed that having a midwife/consultant experienced in breech delivery was essential to a successful outcome, as was the decision to opt for a natural delivery, with minimal intervention.

On my due date, we went out to dinner with some old family friends over from America – John, who had been born breech, his wife, Ruth, whose first child had been born breech, and my parents, whose second child (my sister) had been born breech – I took this as a good omen.

The next day, I had my midwife's appointment and she referred me to a consultant, as I was now overdue. I was given an appointment the following day. All night, I rehearsed arguments to put forward to the consultant I was convinced was going to talk me out of a natural delivery. At the hospital, I was immediately reassured to see an older consultant, who was quick to tell me that he had been trained to deliver breech babies, and that he saw no reason why I should not be allowed to try for a natural delivery. He also said that it was a shame that there were not more people prepared/allowed to do this. He said that with twins, one was often in a breech position, and that there were always going to be occasions in the delivery suite, when babies present breech unexpectedly, too late for anything other than a natural delivery to take place. As caesareans have become routine, few people have seen a natural breech delivery, and this could result in mistakes being made when no other options were available.

Spicy curries did not work and seven days later, I was still waiting and desperate to go into spontaneous labour. We went for a long walk in the park, on a beautiful summer's day. That afternoon, I felt the unmistakable tightening sensation in my stomach, signalling the start of labour.

On arrival at the delivery suite, we were shown into a room, and the midwife was very supportive, saying it was becoming unusual for people to want natural births. She explained that the hospital's policy did not allow midwives to deliver breech babies, and that they (the midwives) would need to assist a consultant.

I sat on the birth ball, asking Mat to rub my back when the contractions came, the contractions which already felt far more intense than they had when Oscar was born. Feeling hungry and thirsty, we walked to the hospital's vending machine, when my waters broke, all over the hospital corridor. The labour seemed to be progressing well, and apart from intermittent monitoring of the baby's heart, we were left to ourselves.

After what seemed a long time waiting, I suddenly felt an uncontrollable urge to push, followed by the emergence of a pair of feet. Mat rushed off to find the midwife. I was told to wait until the consultant ensured I was fully dilated, which fortunately I was.

The next stage happened very quickly, and after a few pushes, I was told I had delivered a healthy baby girl – 8lb 5oz, and Mat was able to cut her cord, before she was checked over by the paediatrician. When she was given back to me, she was very alert, and took straight to breastfeeding. Being wheeled into the ward, in the small hours of the morning, I found that we had become the focus of attention, everyone asking if it was me who had given birth to the breech baby.

For the rest of the night, as I gazed down at Ruby, feeding and sleeping, I was overwhelmed by emotions, relieved that everything had gone well and proud of us, for having achieved what we both wanted. My only regret was that I had not been given the option of a natural birth as soon as I had discovered she was breech. As a result, I had spent an anxious month, trying to get her to turn round, thinking I would have to have a caesarean if she did not. I was not able to fully enjoy this special time with Oscar, giving him my undivided attention, before he had to share me with his baby sister.

We were discharged from hospital the next morning – our stay having cost considerably less than a caesarean would have done, and since then, my upside down baby has continued to go from strength to strength.

Ruth recently told us:

> Since then I have read of and heard of several other women who had had breech babies and found themselves being forced into undergoing a caesarean, when they had been keen for a natural delivery. I do not want to advocate a natural delivery instead of a caesarean every time a baby presents breech, as having midwives/consultants experienced in breech delivery is necessary to a successful outcome, along with trying for a natural delivery with no intervention. There are always going to be occasions when babies present breech unexpectedly, at the last minute, when it is too late for anything but a natural delivery to take place, and often one twin is found to be breech. If everyone routinely prescribes caesareans for breech births, and experience in delivery of breech babies is essential for their safe arrival, then how are the practitioners going to get the experience if they never see live breech births? Interestingly enough, the outcome of the breech term trial (which is why consultants tell you you must have a caesarean) is not as onerous as they would have you believe. It is not just the financial costs of caesareans versus natural deliveries to consider – many women feel robbed if they are not allowed to experience natural birth, or if they feel that they do not have a choice in the matter.

We hope that the information in this book together with the birth stories from women who have successfully avoided unnecessary caesareans give you hope and encouragement to see that vaginal birth is a safe and viable option for you in most cases. On pages 89–90 you will find a list of useful contacts – organisations and websites where you can find more information and the practical support you may need. Good luck!

References

1   BirthChoiceUK 2007, www.birthchoiceuk.com [Accessed 03 July 2007].

2   Churchill, H., Savage, W. and Francome, C. *Caesarean Birth in Britain, Revised and Updated*, London: Middlesex University Press, 2006.

3   Burrows, L.J. 'Maternal morbidity associated with vaginal versus caesarean delivery', *Obstetrics & Gynecology* 2004, 3:907–12.

4   Hillan, E. 'Postoperative morbidity following caesarean delivery', *Journal of Advanced Nursing* 1995, 22:1035–42.

5   Churchill, H., Savage, W. and Francome, C. *Caesarean Birth in Britain, Revised and Updated*, London: Middlesex University Press, 2006.

6   Zanardo, V. 'Neonatal respiratory morbidity risk and mode of delivery at term: influence of timing of elective caesarean delivery', *Acta Paediatrica* 2004, 93:643–7.

7   Hillan, E. 'Research and audit, women's views of caesarean section' in Roberts, H. (ed.) *Women's Health Matters*, London: Routledge, 1992.

8   Churchill, H. *Caesarean Birth: Experience, Practice and History*, Manchester: Books for Midwives Press, 1997.

9   Churchill, H., Savage, W. and Francome, C. *Caesarean Birth in Britain, Revised and Updated*, London: Middlesex University Press, 2006.

10   Mathur, G.P., Pandey, P.K., Mathur, S. and Sharma, S. 'Breastfeeding in babies delivered by cesarean section', *Indian Paediatrics* 1993, 30:1285–90.

11   Ever-Hadani, P., Seidman, D.S., Manor, O. and Harlap, S. 'Breast feeding in Israel: Maternal factors associated with choice and duration', *Journal of Epidemiology and Community Health* 1994, 48:281–5.

12   Menghetti, E., Marulli, P., Mucedola, G. and Montaleone, M. 'The nutrition of the nursing mother in light of a study of 200 new mothers', *Minerva Pediatrica* 1994, 46:331–4.

13   Churchill, H. *Caesarean Birth: Experience, Practice and History*, Manchester: Books for Midwives Press, 1997.

14   Churchill, H., Savage, W. and Francome, C. *Caesarean Birth in Britain, Revised and Updated*, London: Middlesex University Press, 2006.

15   Savage, W. and Francome, C. 'British consultants' attitudes to caesareans', *Journal of Obstetrics & Gynaecology: the Journal of the Institute of Obstetrics and Gynaecology* 2007, 27:354–9.

16   Churchill, H., Savage, W. and Francome, C. *Caesarean Birth in Britain, Revised and Updated*, London: Middlesex University Press, 2006.

17   Thomas, J. and Paranjothy, S. *Royal College of Obstetricians and Gynaecologists Clinical Effectiveness Support Unit: National Sentinel Caesarean Section Audit Report*, London: RCOG Press, 2001.

18   Ibid.

19   Churchill, H. and Savage, W. *Vaginal Birth After Caesarean*, London: Middlesex University Press, 2008.

20 WHO (World Health Organisation), 'Appropriate technology for birth', *The Lancet* 1985, 2:436–7.

21 Thomas, J. and Paranjothy, S. *Royal College of Obstetricians and Gynaecologists Clinical Effectiveness Support Unit: National Sentinel Caesarean Section Audit Report*, London: RCOG Press, 2001.

22 Churchill, H. and Savage, W. *Vaginal Birth After Caesarean*, London: Middlesex University Press, 2008.

23 Enkin, M., Keirse, M.J.N.C., Neilson, J., Renfrew, M. and Neilson, J. *A Guide to Effective Care in Pregnancy and Childbirth, third edition*, Oxford: Oxford University Press, 2000.

24 Phipps, M., Watabe, B. and Clemons, J.L. 'Risk factors for bladder injury during caesarean delivery', *Obstetrics and Gynecology* 2005, 105:156–60.

25 Macones, G.A., Peipert, J. and Nelson, D.B. 'Maternal complications with vaginal birth after cesarean delivery: A Multicenter study', *American Journal of Obstetrics and Gynecology* 2005, 193:1656–62.

26 Ibid.

27 Gould, D. 'Emergency Obstetric Hysterectomy – an increasing incidence', *Journal of Obstetrics and Gynaecology* 1999, 19:580–3.

28 Fogelson, N.S., Menard, M.K. and Hulsey, T. 'Neonatal impact of elective repeat cesarean delivery at term: A comment on patient choice cesarean delivery', *American Journal of Obstetrics and Gynecology* 2005, 192:1433–6.

29 MacDorman, M.F., Declercq, E. and Menacker, F. 'Infant and Neonatal Mortality for Primary Cesarean and Vaginal Births to Women with "No Indicated Risk" United States, 1998–2001 Birth Cohorts', *Birth* 2006, 33:175–82.

30 Villar, J., Valladares, E.L. and Wojdyla, D. 'WHO 2005 global survey on maternal and perinatal health research group. Caesarean delivery rates and pregnancy outcomes: the 2005 WHO global survey on maternal and perinatal health in Latin America', *The Lancet* 2006, 367:1819–29.

31 Wen, S.W., Rusen, I.D. and Walker, M. 'Comparison of maternal mortality and morbidity between trial of labor and elective cesarean section among women with previous cesarean delivery', *American Journal of Obstetrics and Gynecology* 2004, 1263–9.

32 DoH (Department of Health), *Why mothers die 2000–2002. Report on confidential enquiries into maternal mortality in the United Kingdom,* table 1.11, London: RCOG Press, 2004.

33 MacDonald, D., Grant, A. and Sheridan-Pereira, M. 'The Dublin randomised controlled trial of intrapartum fetal heart rate monitoring', *American Journal of Obstetrics & Gynecology* 1985, 152:524–39.

34 Author not given, 'Electronic Fetal Heart Rate Monitoring: Research Guidelines for Interpretation', *American Journal of Obstetrics and Gynecology* 1997, 177:1385–90.

35 O'Driscoll, K. 'Active management of labour and cephalopelvic disproportion', *Journal of Obstetrics & Gynaecology of the British Commonwealth* 1970, 77:385–9.

36   Thornton, J.G. and Lilford, R.J. 'Active management of labour: current knowledge and research issues', *British Medical Journal* 1994, 309:336–9.

37   NICE (National Institute for Clinical Excellence), *Caesarean Section, National Collaborating Centre for Women's and Children's Health, Clinical Guideline*, London: RCOG Press, 2004, p.49.

38   Pattinson, R.E. 'Pelvimetry for fetal cephalic presentation at term', *Cochrane Database Syst Rev* 13:2001.

39   Thorpe–Beeston, J.G., Banfield, P.J. and Saunders, N.J. 'Outcome of breech delivery at term', *British Medical Journal* 1992, 305:746–7.

40   Collea, J.V., Chein, C. and Quilligan, E.J. 'The randomized management of term frank breech presentation: a study of 208 cases', *American Journal of Obstetrics & Gynecology* 1980, 137:235–44.

41   Hannah, M.E. 'Planned caesarean section versus planned vaginal delivery for breech presentation at term: a randomised multicentre trial', *The Lancet* 2000, 356:1375–83.

42   van Roosmalen, J. and van Rosendaal, F. 'There is still room for disagreement about vaginal delivery of breech infants at term', *British Journal of Obstetrics & Gynaecology* 2002, 109:967–9.

43   Pradhan, P., Mohajer, M. and Deshpande, S. 'Outcome of term breech births: 10 year experience at a District General Hospital', *British Journal of Obstetrics & Gynaecology* 2005, 112:218–22.

44   Hofmeyer, G.J. 'External version facilitation for breech presentation term', *Cochrane Database Syst Rev: Issue 3*, 2001.

45   RCOG (Royal College of Obstetricians and Gynaecologists), *Management of Breech presentation, Guideline No. 20*, London: RCOG, 2001.

46   Hofmeyer, G.J. 'External version facilitation for breech presentation term', *Cochrane Database Syst Rev: Issue 3*, 2001.

47   Waites, B. *Breech Birth*, London & New York: Free Association Books, 2003.

48   Cronk, M. 'Hands off that breech!' *Aims Journal* 2005, 17:1–3.

49   Redman, C. and Walker, I. *Pre-eclampsia: The facts – the hidden threat to pregnancy*, Oxford: Oxford University Press, 1992.

50   Berkowitz, G.S. 'Delayed childbirth and the outcome of pregnancy', *New England Journal of Medicine* 1990, 322:659–64.

51   Al-Turki, H.A. 'The outcome of pregnancy in elderly primigravidas', *Saudi Medical Journal* 2003, 24:1230–3.

52   ONS (Office for National Statistics), *Child Health Statistics, 2nd edition*, London: The Stationery Office, 2000.

53   GSS (Government Statistical Service), *NHS Maternity Statistics, England: 1989–90 to 1994–95*, London: HMSO, 1998.

54   POST (Parliamentary Office of Science and Technology), *Postnote, Caesarean Sections*, No.184, 2002.

55   Office of Health Economics Press release, 26 February 2007, 'How the UK NHS expenditure and staffing has changed, Rising UK birth rates and causes of increasing numbers of caesarean deliveries':

http://www.ohe.org/lib/liDownload/524/Comp%20PRESS%20RELEASE.pdf?CFID
=35581&CFTOKEN=87342393&jsessionid=f830153f80944c4e5b55 [Accessed
17 July 2007].

56 Martel, M. 'Maternal age and primary caesarean section rates: a multivariate
analysis', *American Journal of Obstetrics & Gynecology* 1987, 156:305–8.

57 Bell, J.S. 'Do obstetric complications explain high caesarean section rates among
women over 30? A retrospective analysis', British Medical Journal 2001,
322:894–5.

58 Ibid.

59 Thomas, J. and Paranjothy, S. *Royal College of Obstetricians and Gynaecologists
Clinical Effectiveness Support Unit: National Sentinel Caesarean Section Audit
Report*, London: RCOG Press, 2001.

60 SPCERH (Scottish Programme for Clinical Effectiveness in Reproductive Health),
*Expert Advisory Group on Caesarean Section in Scotland, Report and
Recommendations to the Chief Medical Officer of the Scottish Executive Health
Department*, 2001.

61 Social Trends 33 2001, 'Maternities with multiple births: by age of mother at
childbirth'. URL:
www.statistics.gov.uk/StatBase/ssdataset.app?vlnk=6378&Pos=&ColRank=2&Ran
k=816 [Accessed 20 May 2005].

62 Smith, G.C.S. 'Birth order, gestational age, and risk of delivery related perinatal
death in twins: retrospective cohort study', *British Medical Journal* 2002,
325:1004.

63 Rydhstrom, H., Ingemarsson, I., Ohrlander, S. 'Lack of correlation between a
high caesarean section rate and improved prognosis for low-birthweight twins
(<2500g)', *British Journal of Obstetrics & Gynaecology* 1990, 97:229–33.

64 Wildschut, H.U. 'Planned abdominal compared with planned vaginal birth in
triplet pregnancies', *British Journal of Obstetrics and Gynaecology* 1995,
102:292–6.

65 Mahoney, E. *Stand & Deliver and Other Brilliant Ways to Give Birth*, London:
Thorsons, 2005.

66 Walker, R. 'Increasing caesarean section rates: exploring the role of culture in an
Australian Community', *Birth* 2004, 31:117–24.

67 Thomas, J. and Paranjothy, S. *Royal College of Obstetricians and Gynaecologists
Clinical Effectiveness Support Unit: National Sentinel Caesarean Section Audit
Report*, London: RCOG Press, 2001.

68 DoH (Department of Health) 2003, 'Different models of maternity care: an
evaluation of the roles of primary health care workers'. URL:
www.dh.gov.uk/PolicyAndGuidance/ResearchAndDevelopment/ResearchAnd
[Accessed 12 May 2005].

69 DoH (Department of Health) 2003, 'Infant Feeding Initiative. A Report Evaluating
the Breastfeeding Practice Projects 1999–2002'. URL:
www.doh.gov/infantfeeding [Accessed 25 April 2005].

70 DoH (Department of Health) 2003, 'Different models of maternity care: an
evaluation of the roles of primary health care workers'. URL:

www.dh.gov.uk/PolicyAndGuidance/ResearchAndDevelopment/ResearchAnd [Accessed 12 May 2005].

71 HoC (House of Commons) 2003, 'Select Committee on Health Ninth Report'. URL: www.parliament.the-stationery-office.co.uk/pa/cm200203/cmselect/ cmhealth/7 [Accessed 19 May 2005]. Parliamentary copyright material is reproduced with the permission of the Controller of Her Majesty's Stationery Office on behalf of Parliament. Section 2, p.1.

72 NICE National Institute for Clinical Excellence, *Caesarean Section, National Collaborating Centre for Women's and Children's Health, Clinical Guideline*, London: RCOG Press, 2004.

73 Churchill, H. *Caesarean Birth: Experience, Practice and History*, Manchester: Books for Midwives Press, 1997.

74 Chamberlain, G. *Home Births: The report of the 1994 confidential enquiry by the National Birthday Trust Fund*, Carnforth: Parthenon Press, 1997.

75 HoC (House of Commons) 2003, 'Select Committee on Health Ninth Report'. URL: www.parliament.the-stationery-office.co.uk/pa/cm200203/cmselect/ cmhealth/7 [Accessed 19 May 2005]. Parliamentary copyright material is reproduced with the permission of the Controller of Her Majesty's Stationery Office on behalf of Parliament. Section 3, p.3.

76 Maternity Services, *Government response to the second report from the Health Select Committee, Cmmd. 2018,* London: HMSO, 1992.

77 Thewlis, S. 'Midwives and Home Birth', *Nursing and Midwives Circular 8–2006*, p.4. URL: http://www.nmc_uk.org/aFrameDisplay.aspx?DocumentID=1680 [Accessed 8 April 2007].

78 The Portland Hospital 2006, www.theportlandhospital.com/maternity-statistics.asp [Accessed 18 July 2007].

79 Churchill, H., Savage, W. and Francome, C. *Caesarean Birth in Britain, Revised and Updated*, London: Middlesex University Press, 2006.

80 HoC (House of Commons) 2003, 'Select Committee on Health Ninth Report'. URL: www.parliament.the-stationery-office.co.uk/pa/cm200203/cmselect cmhealth/7 [Accessed 19 May 2005]. Parliamentary copyright material is reproduced with the permission of the Controller of Her Majesty's Stationery Office on behalf of Parliament. Section 4, p.6.

Abbreviations

AIMS	Association for Improvements in Maternity Services
ALSO	Advanced Life Support Obstetrics
CTG	Cardiotocograph
EFM	Electronic fetal monitor(ing)
HBAC	Vaginal birth at home after previous caesarean (HBA2C is a home vaginal birth after two caesareans)
HELLP	Haemolysis elevated liver enzymes and low platelet count syndrome
IVF	In vitro fertilisation
NHS	National Health Service
NICE	National Institute for Clinical Excellence
OP	Occipito-posterior
PCT	Primary care trust
PET	Pre-eclampsia
PMR	Perinatal mortality rate
RCT	Randomised controlled trial
TENS	Transcutaneous Electrical Nerve Stimulation
US/USA	United States of America
VBAC	Vaginal birth after caesarean

Glossary

Admission Trace – The 20- or 30-minute CTG recording given to women on their admission to hospital.

Amniotomy – Artificial rupture of the fetal membranes to induce or hasten labour.

Antenatal – Before birth.

Cardiotocograph (CTG) – See *electronic fetal heart monitor.*

Cephalic presentation – The normal position for a baby before labour begins: head down.

Cerebral palsy – Brain damage occurring either before or during birth resulting in physical and, less often, mental disability.

Diabetes – A disorder where the body's way of dealing with sugar is defective, which manifests itself with increased urine production.

Domino system of care – See Appendix A.

Eclampsia – The severe form of pre-eclampsia (see below) when a mother has fits or convulsions. It is also often associated with blood-clotting problems.

Effaced/Effacing – Shortening, softening and thinning of the cervix during labour.

Elective caesarean – Planned caesarean (i.e. before labour has commenced).

Electronic fetal heart monitor – A machine which collects information about a baby's heartbeat using ultrasound from a belt on the mother's abdomen or a clip fastened to the baby's head ('fetal scalp electrode'). The information is printed out continuously onto a strip of paper (a 'trace') which hospital staff can read during labour and which forms part of the permanent record of the birth.

Endometritis – Inflammation of the lining of the uterus (endometrium), often occurring as postpartum infection.

External cephalic version – The procedure whereby an obstetrician attempts to turn a breech baby into a more favourable position before labour begins.

HELLP Syndrome – 'Haemolysis elevated liver enzymes and low platelet count syndrome'. A serious disorder of pregnancy characterised by a great reduction in the number of platelets, haemolysis, abnormal liver function tests and sometimes, hypertension. In the most severe cases, it may require delivery of the baby before term.

Herpes simplex – An acute viral condition characterised by clusters of watery blisters on the genitals or on the lips. There is a risk of transferring the virus to the baby if genital herpes are present at birth. A caesarean may be recommended to avoid this risk.

In vitro fertilisation – A process of artificial conception whereby eggs are gathered from the woman's ovaries and mixed with the man's sperm in a dish before being implanted back into the woman's womb.

Malpresentation – Referring to babies in the womb meaning not in the usual vertex (head-down) position for birth.

Medicalised – A sociological term meaning aspects of human life (pregnancy and birth for example) that have been brought under medical scrutiny and turned into a medical problem, a disease or illness even.

Occipito-posterior position – A cephalic (head-down) presentation of the fetus with the back of the head turned to the right (right occipito-posterior, ROP) or to the left (left occipito-posterior, LOP).

Oxytocin – The hormone which causes the uterus to contract during labour. It is also released by the woman's body during orgasm and breastfeeding.

Perinatal – The period between twenty-four weeks of pregnancy and seven days after birth.

Perinatal mortality ratio/rate (PMR or PNMR) – The rate (usually expressed per 1,000) of babies dying between twenty-four weeks of pregnancy and seven days after birth.

Pre-eclampsia – A condition arising during pregnancy which, if left untreated, could cause fits in the mother and cut off the oxygen supply to her baby. Symptoms are increased blood pressure often accompanied by swelling of the limbs and protein in the urine. The only 'cure' is delivery of the baby, often by caesarean if the condition is severe and the cervix unfavourable.

Primary caesarean – A woman's first caesarean.

Singleton – A single baby (that is, not twins).

TENS (Transcutaneous Electrical Nerve Stimulation) – A low-tech form of pain relief which a woman can use on herself by means of a small, hand-held, battery-operated machine. TENS works by means of two pairs of electrodes taped to the woman's lower back, transmitting a signal which works in two ways to reduce the level of pain from contractions. The first is by interfering with the signals being transmitted to the brain; the second by promoting the production of the body's naturally occurring pain-killers, endorphins.

Term breech – A baby presenting at breech at term.

Thromboembolism – Obstruction of a blood vessel with material carried by the blood stream from the site of origin to plug another vessel.

Unstable lie – Where the baby does not stay in one position in the uterus.

Version – See external cephalic version.

Further information for parents

Balaskas, J. *Active Birth: The new approach to giving birth naturally*, revised edition, Harvard Common Press, 1992.
How to prepare for an active birth.

Churchill, H. and Savage, W. *Vaginal Birth After Caesarean: The VBAC Handbook*, Middlesex University Press, 2008.
A resource for women who have had a caesarean and want to achieve vaginal birth.

Enkin, M., Keirse, M., Neilson, J., Crowther, C., Dudley, L., Hodnett, E. and Hofmeyr, J. *A Guide to Effective Care in Pregnancy and Childbirth*, third edition, Oxford University Press, 2000.
A summary of research findings on all aspects of maternity care.

MIDIRS (Midwives Information and Resource Service) Leaflets for patients and professionals: *Caesarean Birth and VBAC*, Informed Choice Series, Leaflet No 17.
A short leaflet containing information on caesarean birth in general and a section on VBAC available through MIDIRS. Address: MIDIRS, Freepost, 9 Elmdale Road, Clifton, Bristol, BS8 1ZZ. Website: www.infochoice.org

Organisations

Association for Improvements in the Maternity Services (AIMS)
Helpline: 0870 765 1433
Website: www.aims.org
Voluntary pressure group offering support with regard to parents' rights, complaints procedures and choices for maternity care.

National Childbirth Trust
Alexandra House, Oldham Terrace, Acton, London W3 6NH
Tel: 0870 770 3236
Website: www.nct.org.uk
Email: enquiries@nct.org.uk

Over 320 local branches throughout the United Kingdom with networks of informal support, including antenatal teachers, breastfeeding counsellors and postnatal support groups. Local branches will have information about what sort of service to expect from local maternity services and will have details of local support groups for home birth and for women who have had or are expecting to have a caesarean. ParentAbility provides information for parents with disabilities or medical conditions and puts them in touch with each other.

VBAC Information and Support, c/o Caroline Spear, 50 Whiteways, North Bersted, Bognor Regis, West Sussex, PO22 9AS
Tel: 01243 868440

Network of volunteers offering information and support for women wanting a vaginal birth after a previous caesarean.

Websites

www.birthchoiceuk.com

Explains options and gives information to help you make choices about where to have your baby and who should look after you in labour.

www.childbirth.org

Promotes birth as a natural process. Provides links to other useful sites.

www.homebirth.org.uk

Information about home birth for parents and professionals, including a page on VBAC.

www.nct.org.uk

NCT offers support in pregnancy, childbirth and early parenthood. They aim to give every parent the chance to make informed choices.

Appendix A – six types of care for birth

The table overleaf aims to explain to women the main features of the different packages of maternity care on offer in Britain. At first sight, the table may seem complex, but it is not nearly as complicated as the system which it aims to explain! By choosing one of the packages of care in the first column on the left, you can discover its main features by reading horizontally across to the right. If you are particularly interested in one feature of care such as giving birth at home, for example, you can choose the column entitled 'Place of birth' and read down vertically to see which packages of care offer this option.

Package of care	Who gives antenatal care?	Where is antenatal care given?	Place of birth	Who delivers the baby?	Essential features of the package	With whom to book your care
Home birth	Community or independent midwives and/or GP	At home or in GP surgery or community clinic	At home	Community or independent midwife with cover from GP or hospital	All your care takes place at home and you have the chance to get to know the midwife or small team of midwives, one of whom will attend your birth	Community midwives or GP or via supervisor of midwives
Total hospital care	Hospital or community midwives and hospital doctors	Hospital antenatal clinic	Hospital	Hospital midwife; in a teaching hospital a student midwife or doctor under supervision; cover from obstetricians	All care conducted by hospital-based midwives and doctors directly responsible to consultant obstetricians whose (individual) policies will determine the way care is provided	GP or direct with the hospital: ring and ask for the antenatal clinic
Shared care	GP, often assisted by community midwife, and hospital midwives and doctors	GP surgery and hospital antenatal clinic	Hospital	As above	Similar to a hospital birth except that many routine antenatal appointments are with your GP or community midwives. Many women welcome this more personal form of care which may mean less travel and shorter waiting times.	Your GP or, if s/he does not offer the service, or, if you prefer, with another GP
Domino scheme	Community midwives (can be combined with shared care from GP)	At home or GP surgery or midwives' clinic in community or in hospital	Hospital	Community midwife; cover from obstetricians	All care is given by a community midwife or small team of community midwives, so you get to know the person who will attend your delivery, provided there are flexible working patterns. An important bonus is that a community midwife assesses you in labour at home. Six-hour discharge if you want.	Your GP or with the community midwives: ring them at your local maternity unit
Team midwifery or caseload midwifery scheme	Small team of midwives working in hospital and in the community	At home or midwives' clinic in community or in hospital	At home or in hospital	Team midwife; cover as above	You receive individualised care from a small team you get to know well	The team via your GP or the local hospital
Birth centre (also known as 'midwife-led units', 'birthing centres', 'maternity hospitals' or 'GP units')	Community midwives	At the birth centre	Isolated unit or unit alongside district general hospital	Community midwives; cover from GP or district general hospital	A personal form of care with a high rate of continuity of carer. A comfortable, low-tech environment. Available to women with 'low-risk' pregnancies, i.e. no potential complications. There are a number of NHS centres in the UK. There are some private birth centres run by independent midwives for those who wish to pay.	Your GP or another GP or with the community midwives

Appendix B – the latest British hospital data

Data collected from published sources and made publicly available by
www.BirthChoiceUK.com.

England, Caesarean Rates by Hospital 2006

Hospital	Caesarean Rate (%)
Airedale General Hospital	30.0
Alexandra Hospital, Redditch – data combined with Worcestershire Royal Hospital	26.0
Arrowe Park Hospital, Birkenhead	24.0
Barnet General Hospital	23.0
Barnsley District General Hospital	18.0
Basildon Hospital	24.0
Bassetlaw District General Hospital, Worksop	23.0
Bedford Hospital	24.0
Birmingham Heartlands Hospital – data combined with Solihull Hospital	23.0
Birmingham Women's Hospital	24.0
Bradford Royal Infirmary	20.0
Burnley General Hospital	23.0
Calderdale Royal Hospital	23.0
Chase Farm Hospital, Enfield	28.0
Chelsea and Westminster Hospital	34.0
Cheltenham General Hospital – data combined with Gloucestershire Royal Hospital	23.0
Chesterfield and North Derbyshire Royal Hospital	19.0
City Hospital, Birmingham	23.0
Colchester General Hospital	27.0
Conquest Hospital, St Leonards on Sea, data combined with Eastbourne District General Hospital	23.0
Countess of Chester Hospital	26.0
County Hospital, Hereford	26.0
Cumberland Infirmary, Carlisle – data combined with West Cumberland Hospital, Whitehaven	23.0

Hospital	Caesarean Rate (%)
Darent Valley Hospital, Dartford	24.0
Darlington Memorial Hospital	22.0
Derby City General Hospital	24.0
Derriford Hospital, Plymouth	21.0
Dewsbury and District Hospital	22.0
Diana Princess of Wales Hospital, Grimsby – data combined with Scunthorpe General Hospital	19.0
Doncaster Royal Infirmary	20.0
Dorset County Hospital	26.0
Ealing Hospital, Southall	27.0
East Surrey Hospital, Redhill	30.0
Eastbourne District General Hospital – data combined with Conquest Hospital, St Leonards on Sea	23.0
Elizabeth Garrett Anderson Hospital	29.0
Epsom General Hospital – data combined with St Helier Hospital, Carshalton	28.0
Fairfield General Hospital, Bury – data combined with Rochdale Infirmary, North Manchester General Hospital, The Royal Oldham Hospital	22.0
Friarage Hospital, Northallerton	21.0
Frimley Park Hospital	24.0
Furness General Hospital – data combined with Royal Lancaster Infirmary	21.0
Gloucestershire Royal Hospital – data combined with Cheltenham General Hospital	23.0
Good Hope Hospital, Sutton Coldfield	24.0
Great Western Hospital, Swindon – see under The Great Western	
Harrogate District Hospital	27.0
Heatherwood Hospital, Ascot – data combined with Wexham Park Hospital, Slough	25.0
Hillingdon Hospital, Uxbridge	24.0
Hinchingbrooke Hospital, Huntingdon	23.0
Homerton Hospital	24.0
Hope Hospital, Salford	23.0

Hospital	Caesarean Rate (%)
Horton Hospital, Banbury	24.0
Huddersfield Royal Infirmary	20.0
Hull Royal Infirmary	21.0
Ipswich Hospital	26.0
James Cook University Hospital, Middlesbrough	21.0
James Paget Hospital, Great Yarmouth	22.0
John Radcliffe Hospital, Oxford – see under The John Radcliffe	
Kettering General Hospital	24.0
King George Hospital, Ilford	22.0
King's College Hospital, London	26.0
Kings Mill Centre, Sutton-in-Ashfield	17.0
Kingston Hospital	27.0
Leeds General Infirmary – data combined with St James's University Hospital, Leeds	20.0
Leicester General Hospital – data combined with Leicester Royal Infirmary	21.0
Leighton Hospital, Crewe	20.0
Lincoln County Hospital	22.0
Lister Hospital, Stevenage – data combined with Queen Elizabeth II Hospital, Welwyn	23.5
Liverpool Women's Hospital	23.0
Luton and Dunstable Hospital	24.0
Macclesfield District General Hospital	26.0
Maidstone Hospital	27.0
Manor Hospital, Walsall	28.0
Mayday Hospital, Croydon	24.0
Medway Maritime Hospital, Gillingham	24.0
Milton Keynes General Hospital	26.0
New Cross Hospital, Wolverhampton	26.0
Newham Hospital	28.0
Norfolk And Norwich University Hospital	24.0
North Devon District Hospital, Barnstaple	25.0
North Hampshire Hospital, Basingstoke	22.0

Hospital	Caesarean Rate (%)
North Manchester General Hospital – data combined with Rochdale Infirmary, Fairfield General Hospital, Bury, The Royal Oldham Hospital	23.0
North Middlesex Hospital	20.0
North Staffordshire Hospital, Stoke on Trent	25.0
North Tyneside General Hospital – data combined with Wansbeck General hospital	21.0
Northampton General Hospital	27.0
Northwick Park Hospital, Harrow	30.0
Nottingham City Hospital	18.0
Nuneaton Maternity Hospital	25.0
Ormskirk District General Hospital – data combined with Christiana Hartley Maternity Unit, Southport	22.0
Pembury Hospital, Tunbridge Wells	27.0
Peterborough District Hospital	22.0
Pilgrim Hospital, Boston	20.0
Pontefract General Infirmary	17.0
Poole Hospital	26.0
Portland Hospital – see under The Portland Hospital (Private)	
Princess Alexandra Hospital, Harlow	27.0
Princess Anne Hospital, Southampton	22.0
Princess Royal Hospital, Haywards Heath – data combined with Royal Sussex County Hospital, Brighton	29.0
Princess Royal University Hospital, Orpington	29.0
Queen Charlotte's and Chelsea Hospital	34.0
Queen Elizabeth Hospital, Gateshead	24.0
Queen Elizabeth Hospital, Kings Lynn	20.0
Queen Elizabeth Hospital, Woolwich	21.0
Queen Elizabeth II Hospital, Welwyn – data combined with Lister Hospital, Stevenage	23.5
Queen Elizabeth the Queen Mother Hospital – data combined with Kent and Canterbury Hospital, William Harvey Hospital, Ashford	20.0
Queen Mary's Hospital, Sidcup	28.0
Queen's Hospital, Burton upon Trent	25.0

Hospital	Caesarean Rate (%)
Queen's Park Hospital, Blackburn	21.0
Rochdale Infirmary – data combined with Fairfield General Hospital, Bury, North Manchester General Hospital, The Royal Oldham Hospital	22.0
Rosie Maternity Hospital	28.0
Rotherham District General Hospital	20.0
Royal Albert Edward Infirmary, Wigan	22.0
Royal Berkshire Hospital, Reading	27.0
Royal Bolton Hospital	22.0
Royal Cornwall Hospital, Truro	21.0
Royal Devon and Exeter Hospital	27.0
Royal Free Hospital, Hampstead	30.0
Royal Hallamshire Hospital, Jessop Wing	24.0
Royal Hampshire County Hospital, Winchester	25.0
Royal Lancaster Infirmary – data combined with Furness General Hospital	21.0
Royal London Hospital, Whitechapel	24.0
Royal Oldham Hospital – see under The Royal Oldham Hospital	
Royal Shrewsbury Hospital	15.0
Royal Surrey County Hospital, Guildford	25.0
Royal Sussex County Hospital, Brighton – data combined with Princess Royal Hospital, Haywards Heath	29.0
Royal United Hospital, Bath	21.0
Royal Victoria Infirmary, Newcastle	22.0
Russells Hall Hospital	Data not available
St George's Hospital, Tooting	23.0
St Helier Hospital, Carshalton – data combined with Epsom General Hospital	28.0
St James's University Hospital, Leeds – data combined with Leeds General Infirmary	20.0
St John's Hospital, Chelmsford	29.0
St Mary's Hospital, Isle of Wight	22.0
St Mary's Hospital, Manchester	19.0

Hospital	Caesarean Rate (%)
St Mary's Hospital, Paddington	31.0
St Mary's Hospital, Portsmouth	26.0
St Michael's Hospital, Bristol	23.0
St Peter's Hospital, Chertsey	26.0
St Richard's Hospital, Chichester	25.5
St Thomas' Hospital	27.0
Salisbury District Hospital	26.0
Sandwell District General Hospital, West Bromwich	31.0
Scarborough Hospital	18.0
Scunthorpe General Hospital – data combined with Diana, Princess of Wales Hospital	19.0
Sharoe Green Unit, Royal Preston Hospital	22.0
Solihull Hospital – data combined with Birmingham Heartlands Hospital	23.0
South Tyneside District Hospital	22.0
Southend Hospital	30.0
Southmead Hospital, Bristol	26.0
Staffordshire General Hospital	17.0
Stepping Hill Hospital, Stockport	24.0
Stoke Mandeville Hospital, Aylesbury	24.0
Sunderland Royal Hospital	18.0
Tameside General Hospital, Ashton-under-Lyne	18.0
Taunton and Somerset Hospital	26.0
The Great Western Hospital, Swindon	28.0
The John Radcliffe Hospital, Oxford	19.0
The Portland Hospital (Private)[1]	50.0
The Royal Oldham Hospital – data combined with Rochdale Infirmary, Fairfield General Hospital, Bury, North Manchester General Hospital	22.0
Torbay Hospital	23.0
Trafford General Hospital	22.0
University Hospital of Hartlepool – data combined with University Hospital of North Tees	21.0
University Hospital of North Durham	23.0

Hospital	Caesarean Rate (%)
University Hospital of North Tees – data combined with University Hospital of Hartlepool	21.0
University Hospital, Aintree	Data not available
University Hospital, Lewisham	28.0
University Hospital, Nottingham	22.0
Victoria Hospital, Blackpool	24.0
Walsgrave Hospital	26.0
Wansbeck General Hospital – data combined with North Tyneside General Hospital	21.0
Warrington Hospital	27.0
Warwick Hospital	24.0
Watford General Hospital	26.5
West Cumberland Hospital, Whitehaven – data combined with Cumberland Infirmary, Carlisle	23.0
West Middlesex University Hospital, Isleworth	22.0
West Suffolk Hospital, Bury St Edmunds	28.0
Wexham Park Hospital, Slough – data combined with Heatherwood Hospital, Ascot	25.0
Whipps Cross Hospital, Leytonstone	29.0
Whiston Hospital	23.0
Whittington Hospital, Highgate	26.0
William Harvey Hospital, Ashford – data combined with Kent and Canterbury Hospital, Queen Elizabeth the Queen Mother Hospital	20.0
Worcestershire Royal Hospital – data combined with Alexandra Hospital, Redditch	26.0
Worthing Hospital	22.0
Wycombe Hospital	25.0
Wythenshawe Hospital	28.0
Yeovil District Hospital	22.0
York District Hospital	27.0

1   The Portland Hospital 2006 www.theportlandhospital.com/maternity-statistics.asp [Accessed 18 July 2007]

Northern Ireland, Caesarean Rates by Hospital 2004

Hospital	Caesarean Rate (%)
Altnagelvin Area Hospital	21.4
Antrim	26.5
Causeway Hospital	22.0
Craigavon Area Hospital	31.4
Daisy Hill Hospital, Newry	26.9
Downpatrick Maternity Hospital	Data not available
Erne Hospital, Enniskillen	24.5
Lagan Valley Hospital	21.0
Mater Infirmorum, Belfast	26.4
Mid Ulster Hospital, Magherafelt	15.3
Royal Maternity Hospital, Belfast	31.5
Ulster Hospital, Belfast	21.1

Wales, Caesarean Rates by Hospital 2006

Hospital	Caesarean Rate (%)
Bronglais Hospital, Aberystwyth	30.0
Llandough Hospital	15.0
Nevill Hall Hospital – data combined with Royal Gwent Hospital	27.1
Prince Charles Hospital, Merthyr	34.0
Princess of Wales Hospital, Bridgend	26.1
Royal Glamorgan Hospital, Llantristant	31.5
Royal Gwent Hospital – data combined with Nevill Hall Hospital	27.1
Singleton Hospital, Swansea	30.0
University Hospital of Wales	28.5
West Wales General Hospital, Carmarthen	26.3
Withybush Hospital, Haverfordwest	24.0
Ysbyty Glan Clwyd, Rhyl	25.0
Ysbyty Gwynedd, Bangor	22.7
Ysbyty Wrexham Maelor	24.7

Scotland, Caesarean Rates by Hospital 2005

Hospital	Caesarean Rate (%)
Aberdeen Maternity Hospital	27.6
Ayrshire Central and Maternity Hospital	24.8
Balfour Hospital	21.3
Borders General Hospital	20.7
Caithness General Hospital	31.2
Cresswell Maternity Hospital – data combined with Dumfries and Galloway Royal Infirmary	27.2
Dr. Gray's Hospital, Elgin	13.9
Dumfries and Galloway Royal Infirmary – data combined with Cresswell Maternity Hospital	27.2
Forth Park Maternity Hospital, Kirkcaldy	21.8
Gilbert Bain Memorial Hospital[2]	9.2
Inverclyde Royal Hospital (2004)	18.3
Ninewells Hospital, Dundee	23.6
Perth Royal Infirmary	12.0
Princess Royal Maternity Hospital	27.3
Raigmore Hospital, Inverness	29.9
Royal Alexandra Hospital, Paisley	29.3
Royal Infirmary of Edinburgh	27.8
Southern General Hospital, Glasgow	23.5
St. John's at Howden, Livingston	25.7
Sterling Royal Infirmary	20.1
The Queen Mother's Hospital, Glasgow	30.6
Western Isles Hospital	21.9
Wishaw General Hospital	22.5

2   Emergency CS only

Index